W9-DGT-887

Was Jesus Who He Said He Was?

Michael Green

VINE
BOOKS

Servant Publications
Ann Arbor, Michigan

This edition published in 1989 by Vine Books, an imprint of
Servant Publications especially designed to serve Evangelical
Christians

Published by Servant Books
P.O. Box 8617
Ann Arbor, Michigan 48107

Cover design by Gerald Gawronski

Except where the author has made his own translation,
quotations from the Bible are from the Revised Standard
Version, copyright © 1946, 1952, 1971, 1973, by the Division of
Christian Education, National Council of the Churches of
Christ in the U.S.A. and used by permission.

Printed in the United States of America
ISBN 0-89283-624-5

89 90 91 92 93   10 9 8 7 6 5 4 3 2

Library of Congress Cataloging-in-Publication Data

Contents

To honest agnostics in Oxford
and elsewhere

For Tim and Sarah

Preface

Back in 1968 I wrote a book, *Runaway World*. It attempted to examine the question whether Christian belief is a form of escapism, the religious man's way of escaping from the pressures of modern life, or whether in fact the escapists are really those who are unwilling to face up to the evidence for Jesus.

The book took off in a way which astonished author and publisher alike. It went through many editions and translations. The subject was clearly an important one. The book is dated now, not, I think, in its major themes, but in the many illustrations from the sixties which it employs. So I was asked to revise it. Instead, I have written what amounts to a new book on the same theme. I am convinced that escapism is still the order of the day, only more so than it was in the sixties. I believe now, even more strongly than I did then, that it is in general not the Christians but many non-Christians who are on the run from reality. If you do not believe me, read on.

I should like to express my grateful thanks for the help I have received from Professor Douglas Spanner, Dr John and Dr Sonia Hall, Dr David Cook, Mr David Lee, Mr Richard Henderson and my son Timothy Green. All of these have generously given time in the midst of busy lives to advise me on some area where I should otherwise have made even more mistakes than I have. I appreciate it. The biblical quotations in this book are generally from the Revised Standard Version, but sometimes I have given my own rendering.

A big thank-you, too, to Jane Holloway, my colleague and secretary, who produced superbly accurate copy.

The other day I met an Anglican clergyman who is now planting churches in Chile. *Runaway World* had helped him to faith in Christ, and now he is helping many more. It is my prayer that *Was Jesus Who He Said He Was?* may help some readers to take stock of their lives, to discover the living Christ, and to share that discovery with others.

ESCAPISM

1
Escape routes

In Thomas Hobbes' day life could be described as 'nasty, brutish and short'. Now, over three hundred years later, it is 'nasty, brutish and long'. That is why so many people need to get away from it all.

We live in a day of ever-increasing nuclear threat. The club is growing all the time. One day some fool is going to press the button.

Ours is an age of ever-increasing famine. We have the resources to deal with it, but instead we expend them in creating arsenals of the most terrifying weaponry.

We are running out of oil, so we build a Concorde which makes too much noise, gobbles up fuel, and is unsaleable.

Many young people spend eighteen years of their lives trying to get to college or university; they get there, and find they are unemployed when they leave.

Inflation seems to have become endemic. Is there any point in saving when the value of money erodes so fast? Is it worth working at all?

And what about the silicone chip? Specially designed to increase unemployment and the leisure nobody knows what to do with.

No wonder we need escape routes!

So, we dive headlong into the rat-race. We indulge in extra-marital sex. We take refuge in that stiff drink, and settle down in front of the television. We dream of what we might do if we won a lottery, or if only we could buy that little cottage in the country. We need to get away from it all.

Christian escapism?

The greatest unreality, the most comfortable mirage of our day is commonly thought to be religion. Christianity is all very well for those who like that kind of thing, but of course it is sheer escapism. Running away to a Father-figure in the sky in order to escape from the harsh realities of life in the real world. Christians seem rather dull, rather inept at defending their position, but otherwise indistinguishable from everybody else. Clearly their religion does not make much difference. On the practical level, as well as the intellectual, they are on the run.

No doubt there are escapists in our churches. No doubt some, perhaps many, find religion a cosy little nook to retreat into. I do not for a moment deny that. But I emphatically deny that authentic, full-blooded Christianity is escapism. It provides us with the most credible account of the world and our place as human beings within it. It provides us with the motivation and dynamic for serving our fellow men. It enables us to face the toughest situations with realism, and to die with confidence. It is intensely relevant, because it is the truth.

No doubt that sounds rather brash. We are not accustomed to such confidence in Christian claims. As one young journalist put it:

> England has been officially Christian for more than fifteen hundred years. Our whole culture is based on Christianity. However today it is no longer respectable, or even acceptable, actually to *be* a Christian. This is especially so among people of my own age and type . . . It is not that religion in general is out. Roman Catholics are just all right because one is generally born a Catholic and so cannot do anything about it. Mormons are OK too, not to *be*, but for sociological study purposes. The Eastern religions are very trendy. But as for ordinary God-fearing, Bible-reading, Christ-imitating Christianity – it's plain old-fashioned. You're barmy, a freak, if you believe it in these days.

That young man has put his finger on a most important point:

it is unfashionable to be a Christian. Now there could be two reasons for that. One is that Christianity has been tried and found wanting, so it is stupid to pursue it further. The other is that it has not been tried, at any rate by the people concerned. There was once an open-air preacher who was interrupted by a dirty and dishevelled objector: 'A load of nonsense,' he said. 'Christianity has been around for two thousand years and just look at the state of the world.' The preacher was not abashed. 'And water has been in the world for lots longer than two thousand years,' he replied, 'and just look at the state of your neck.'

Non-Christian escapism?

Could it be like that with our society? There is something very strange about the opposition to Christianity. It is not usually direct or reasoned. It is snide and cynical; it comes with a laugh or a groan. 'You're not one of that lot, are you?' If you doubt it, you have only to go into a pub or a board meeting, a working-men's club or a sports dressing-room, and mention Jesus Christ in a way that shows your allegiance to him – and you can be sure of a hostile reaction. It may show itself in silence or laughter, in rudeness or blasphemy, but the reaction will be hostile all right. Isn't that very odd? On any showing, the life of Jesus and the teaching of Jesus are the best that anyone has ever come up with. On any showing his death is the most famous in history. On any showing he is the most celebrated person that has ever existed, and more people follow him today than ever before – and that is two thousand years after his death. Could it be that he was right in saying 'Light has come into the world, and men love darkness rather than light because their deeds are evil'? Could it be that we are desperate to keep out of his way? Could it be that it is not the Christians but the non-aligned who are on the run, running to maintain their independence, running to avoid the clutches of the Great Lover? Francis Thompson spoke for many escapists when he wrote:

I fled Him, down the nights and down the days;
   I fled Him, down the arches of the years;

11

I fled Him, down the labyrinthine ways
  Of my own mind; and in the mist of tears
I hid from Him, and under running laughter.

And all the time he heard a voice, 'All things betray thee, who betrayest Me', 'Naught shelters thee, who wilt not shelter Me', 'Naught contents thee, who content'st not Me.' It was only when he had given in to the 'Hound of Heaven' that he discovered the mistake he had been making all the time. 'Thou dravest love from thee, who dravest Me.'

Who is on the run? Who needs to find a place in which to shelter from reality? Is it the Christians? Or is it those who are anxious to settle down undisturbed by any such thoughts and make their modest pile and do their own thing? That is the question with which this book is concerned. *Who are the escapists?*

2
Is Christianity a crutch?

'I don't need Christianity. It's just a crutch for weaklings.'

I have often heard a sneer like that. I sometimes wonder how the young person, full of health and scorn, who utters those words, would feel if he went skiing in the Alps and broke his leg. I wonder if his attitude towards crutches might change?

A rescue religion

In one sense, Christianity *is* a crutch. It is for people who are fractured. If ours were a perfect world and if we were perfect people there would be no need for Christianity. But such is not the case. Our world, our lives are fractured by greed and selfishness, lust and cruelty. Don't believe me. Just watch the news or read a newspaper. Christianity is unashamedly a repair religion. It is not for the healthy but for the sick: that's what Jesus said. He knew that there are no healthy. 'There is none righteous, no, not one.' Not even you.

So in this sense Christianity is a crutch. It is designed to enable the incapacitated to walk, the greedy to become generous, the lonely integrated, the miserable happy. And Christians maintain that the wood of which that crutch is fashioned will bear anyone's weight. It is well seasoned. It has been maturing for two thousand years. We shall examine the evidence for that claim later on.

An illusion?

But this crutch argument can have a very different twist to it. The claim is not that Christianity is a crutch in the sense of a support: there is none of us so healthy that we do not need that support, and one of the glories of the Christian church is that it is both a hospital and an army. No, when they say that Christianity is just a crutch they mean that it is puerile, illusory, an imaginary solace for the neurotic, an opiate which is designed to discourage social action.

That is the claim, and it has never been put more forcefully and influentially than by Freud. He wrote several books about it, the most trenchant being *The Future of an Illusion*. Freud regarded the Christian religion as a crutch in the sense of something illusory. It did not correspond to anything in the real world. Christianity had the status of an obsessional neurosis. Christians show the classic neurotic tendency to find comfort in religion, and to seek an authority-figure. They project into the empty heavens a Father-figure derived from their own youth. Such belief is the crutch for weaklings and neurotics. It is an illusion, and it arises from subconscious need for comfort and protection.

Freud's position is exposed to a number of criticisms and has been rejected in general by experts in the field of psychology and the behavioural sciences. But it has been readily accepted by the man in the street and by intelligent people in the arts.

Yes, the man in the street has the impression that Freud has explained Christianity away. But has he? There are certainly neurotic Christians, just as there are neurotic psychiatrists. Some Christians are as obsessive about God as Freud was about sex. However, Freud's assumption that God does not exist, but is the projection of our wishful – or fevered – imagination, needs to be evaluated. His complete neglect of the historical basis of Christianity is most surprising. His generalizations, based on a sample which consisted entirely of the mentally ill, are neither scientific nor convincing. Moreover he isolates those elements in Christianity which fit his theory and neglects others, like love of neighbour, which do not. That makes me uneasy. How about you?

Freud has nevertheless put his finger on a most important issue. Is God an illusion? Is the whole of the Christian story pious make-believe? How are we to tell?

It is important to be clear on one point at the outset. When making judgments about God, psychiatrists are simply giving their own opinion, not the findings of their science. Psychology cannot properly be used either to bolster up Christianity or to discredit it. For psychology is not a prescriptive but a descriptive discipline. It analyses the nature and possible origin of people's beliefs, but it cannot dogmatize on their truth or falsity. This must be established by other criteria. Now it may be that Freud and those who follow him are right in supposing that the Christian belief in the fatherly love of God is a reversion to our childhood father-image which we project into the empty heavens. On the other hand it may be the case that there is a God and that he is best described as Father. Let us try to assess these two answers by applying certain tests. Here are three which seem appropriate.

The test of history

Christianity is a historical religion. To dispose of it, you must first get rid of or explain away its founder. And that is a very difficult thing to do. Various theories have been propounded which attempt to explain Jesus as a myth, but they will not stand up to sharp historical investigation. The folly of all such attempts to sidestep the historical Jesus was exposed long ago by Sir James Frazer, author of *The Golden Bough*. He was no friend to Christianity, yet he wrote:

> The doubts which have been cast on the historical reality of Jesus are in my judgment unworthy of serious attention. Quite apart from the positive evidence of history, the origin of a great moral and religious reform is incredible without the personal existence of a great reformer. To dissolve the founder of Christianity into a myth is as absurd as to do the same with Mohammed, Luther or Calvin.

15

But granted the historicity of Jesus, what are we to make of him? His impact on the world was no illusion. We even date our era from his birth. His life of love and integrity, of courage and insight, unparalleled in the annals of mankind, is no illusion. There is nothing illusory about his claims to share God's nature and character: these claims are widely attested in the documents that have come down to us. They are either true or sheer megalomania. His death was real enough, on the rough gibbet of a Roman cross. The resurrection is examined elsewhere in this book, and it is very hard indeed to dub that as illusory. And certainly nobody could deny the reality of the Christian church. That church sprang into being in the thirties of the first century. Its basic message has not changed, and it has gained adherents in increasing millions down the centuries since then, spreading out into every country and tribe in the world – and most strongly in countries like China and Russia where the opposition is most fierce.

In short, there is no lack of evidence about Jesus of Nazareth. His influence and his followers are very much alive all over the world. The Christian religion is based firmly and squarely upon him. The idea that Christianity is wish-fulfilment or self-delusion is shipwrecked on the solid rock of the historical Jesus.

The test of character

The second test of the validity of Christian experience is character. Wherever this faith has appeared across the world and down the ages it has had the most remarkable effects on the character of those who practised it. It has turned rakes into saints, cheats into honest men, enemies into brothers. It would be remarkable if an illusion produced this effect occasionally; but when you find the same results occurring all the time wherever the gospel goes, irrespective of the background, the intelligence and the nationality of the people concerned, then you have every reason to regard what causes the change as real.

An interesting testimony to this transformation of character comes from a surprising source, Charles Darwin. Commending the work of one Mr Fegan, a preacher in his own village, Darwin said, 'Your services have done more for the village in a few months than all our efforts for many years. We have never been able to reclaim a single drunkard, but through your services I do not know that there is a drunkard left in the village!' As a matter of fact he went a good deal further than this. When he first visited Tierra del Fuego he found the savagery and bestiality of the native inhabitants to be beyond belief. When, some years later, he returned, he was amazed at the difference. During his absence a Christian mission had been at work. The people were transformed by the gospel of Jesus Christ and its social and moral implications. And Darwin became a contributor to that missionary society for the rest of his life.

I was recently in America alongside a clergyman who works in the bars and brothels of an inner-city ghetto. We were leading to Christ one of the really tough customers there who had been resisting the gospel for two years. It was a moving experience. But I could not help thinking of the story of the clergyman himself. When I first met him some years ago he was out of work, estranged from his wife, a severe alcoholic, a chain-smoker, sleeping around with prostitutes, and full of bitterness. In the pit of despair this man turned to Jesus Christ. The transformation is plain for all to see. Try persuading him it is illusory!

If you go to the countries of Peru and Colombia, where the Quechua Indians live, you will see a remarkable thing. That large tribe has the reputation for indolence and fecklessness. Until 1956 they were utterly impervious to all attempts to reach them with the gospel of Christ. But since that date many thousands of them have become believers. The results are startling . They begin to take a pride in their families and homes. They begin to work the land and to bring water to their villages. Drunkenness and adultery have almost disappeared. Literacy has grown, and love and laughter have come in. The government officials have noted the difference with profound respect. That is simply one example of the character-change which the gospel of Jesus

Christ always produces when he is allowed to control the life. Illusion? A crutch? The idea is laughable.

The test of power

This brings us naturally to the third test of the validity of religious experience, the test of power. All that we know about delusions and obsessional neuroses is that they tend towards the disintegration of character, unbalanced behaviour and either the inability to achieve goals, or else the dissipation of energy in some strange byway of living. But Christianity has precisely the opposite effect. It makes people whole.

I think of a person deep in black magic who is now, through the liberation afforded by Christ, free from all that and has become a very different person. I think of radiant Christian believers in Uganda, freed from the hatred of a terrible dictator like President Amin who murdered so many of their families and friends. One who escaped that holocaust by a hair's breadth, Bishop Festo Kivengere, can write a book entitled *I Love Idi Amin* and return to his country to encourage forgiveness and partnership all round. I think of a Christian who had been unjustly imprisoned on Robin Island in South Africa, yet remained full of goodwill to those who put him there. I think of Maasai and Kikuyu in Northern Kenya, hereditary enemies: but those who have become Christians are treating each other as brothers. I think of a man trained for ordination in a college where I used to work. He was not long out of prison, and had a variety of chips on his shoulder. Now he is a happy, integrated and most effective clergyman on a tough housing estate. I think of President Nixon's famous aide, Chuck Colson, who found Christ shortly before the Watergate scandal broke, then pleaded guilty and served his sentence in prison. Colson is now giving his life to reclaiming prisoners for Christ throughout the United States, taking them away in small groups to Fellowship House in Washington, and helping them to go back into their prisons to start Christian groups there. Christianity like that seems to me to pass the test of power with flying colours. There is no illusion, no crutch about it.

18

T. R. Glover, one of the most distinguished historians of a previous generation, wrote: 'The strength of Christian convictions is measured by the forces of disruption and decline they have resisted.' True enough, as one reflects on the persecutions, the changing ideologies, the cynicism from without and the decay from within the church that have beset Christianity down the course of the last nineteen hundred years. For an illusion it is remarkably persistent.

Most illusions fail and fade at the approach of death. If Christianity were indeed an illusion, you would not expect it to stand up very well to this final test. But it does. History has shown repeatedly that Christians die well. Others do also, from time to time: Christians have no monopoly of courage. But there is a certain inner logic when a Christian faces death calmly. He is convinced that death is a defeated foe. He is confident that, because Jesus rose, he will share his life. Having lived with Christ and loved him during a lifetime on earth, the fear of death does not unduly chill him. Perfect love casts out fear. And so you often find Christians dying with joy.

Hermann Lange wrote this from his cell shortly before being executed for his faith by the Nazis. It is quoted, along with many other such letters, in Trevor Huddleston's book *Dying We Live*. Lange tells his parents that two feelings occupied his mind the night before his death. 'I am, first, in a joyous mood,' he wrote, 'and second, filled with great anticipation.' The joy came from 'faith in Christ who has preceded us in death. In him I have put my faith, and precisely today I have faith in him more firmly than ever.' He advised them to turn to the New Testament for consolation. 'Look where you will, everywhere you will find jubilation over the grace that makes us children of God. What can befall a child of God? Of what should I be afraid? On the contrary, rejoice!'

This victory over fear, especially fear of the ultimate horror, death, is one of the great moral triumphs of Christianity. It is inexplicable on the theory of illusions or crutches or auto-suggestion. 'By all psychological law', wrote Dr Crighton Miller, himself a distinguished psychoanalyst, 'the auto-suggestion of fear should be the strongest of all . . .

19

unless some factor other than auto-suggestion is on the side of fearlessness.'

Christ, I suggest, is that other factor on the side of fearlessness. He changes character. He gives power. He is no illusion. Indeed, as if to forestall this very charge he uses a remarkable word of himself in John's Gospel. It is the word *alethinos*. It means real, authentic, as opposed to the bogus and the insubstantial. It is in this sense that Jesus claims to be the authentic vine to quench human thirst, the authentic bread to feed hungry hearts. He claims to be nothing less than the absolute, the authentic, in the world of the relative and the illusory. That claim deserves to be examined with care.

3
What is the Christian claim?

> And God held in his hand
> A small globe. Look, he said.
> The son looked. Far off,
> As through water, he saw
> A scorched land of fierce
> Colour. The light burned
> There; crusted buildings
> Cast their shadows; a bright
> Serpent, a river
> Uncoiled itself, radiant
> With slime.
>
> > On a bare
> Hill a bare tree saddened
> The sky. Many people
> Held out their thin arms
> To it, as though waiting
> For a vanished April
> To return to its crossed
> Boughs. The son watched
> Them. Let me go there, he said.

In that brief poem, 'The Coming', R. S. Thomas has encapsulated the heart of the Christian claim.

It begins with God. It maintains that there is a source of this world and all that is in it, a source beyond ourselves, a source that is personal and yet transcends personality. This

God embodies in his own self the tension we perceive within the world: he is both unity and diversity. God is the source of life. God is the sustainer of life. God is the supreme designer of all there is. God is beyond our understanding. We would never have been able to discover him unaided. Our reason is too puny to pierce his incognito. And our self-centredness is too great for us to try very hard.

Our approach to him being thus excluded, he decided to approach us. All down history he has been reaching out to mankind. He called Abraham to trust and follow him. Abraham did, and became the pioneer of people of faith ever since. From him sprang the Jewish nation, and gradually that nation learnt the holiness and judgment, the love and forgiveness of God. They learnt to uphold the one true God against all the background of religious pluralism. They learnt to trust him through disaster and captivity. But still he was the largely unknown God. Still they sensed the alienation, the distance between themselves and him.

The coming

And so to what R. S. Thomas calls 'The Coming'. Without abandoning his supremacy and control over the world, God came to share our situation. He was not dressed up as man; he was man. He was also God. Not all of God that there is (he spoke of his heavenly Father as greater than he), but all of God we could take in. The Christian claim is not that God was exhaustively embodied in Jesus Christ, but that Jesus gives us a true window into God: that, like an iceberg, what we can see in our firmament, though not the whole berg, is yet all of a piece with the part we cannot see. 'He who has seen me has seen the Father', said Jesus. He was a true and perfect sample of the deity expressed to us in the terms most congenial and comprehensible to us, the terms of a human life.

His teachings, his loving actions, his healings, his miracles, his claims all spring from that basic assumption that in Jesus Christ we have to do with man as he ought to be and also with God as he is. That is what makes him totally unique.

22

That is why Christians are unimpressed by the claims of other faiths. They have indeed some truth in them; otherwise they could never have gained adherents. But theirs is the truth of the gloaming; his is the truth of the blazing sunlight. When the perfect has come, the preparatory and incomplete takes a back seat. From now on we do not have to deal with the unknown God. 'In Christ the whole fulness of deity dwells bodily' (Colossians 2:9).

The cross

Why did Christ bother? Not just to be a great example. Not just to embody the love of God. He came to fashion a bridge over the troubled waters of our alienation and self-centredness. He came to construct a road back to God. He did it in an absolutely astonishing way. He laid down his life for us. The point is this: our human wickedness had cut God off from us. It had formed an impenetrable barrier between the two parties. What Christ did on the cross at Calvary was to break through that barrier. He made a path back to God for people who know they are in the wrong and are prepared to accept forgiveness as a free gift. Why should he need to go to such extremes, we may ask? Simply because forgiveness is never cheap. Our sins hurt God. They outrage his holiness. If he was to remain the moral arbiter of the universe he could not ignore them. But if he acted in judgment on them, as he fittingly might, there would be no hope for any of us. So he became one of us and in our place bore the alienation, the judgment which was our due. That is how much he cares. There is nothing like it in all the world.

The resurrection

Death proved unable to hold him. That seems utterly beyond belief to us because we have never experienced perfection. We know only people in whom evil has gained a real foothold. When they die, they do not rise again. Death has an awful finality about it. But we do not know what it would do to someone who was perfect. There has been only one such.

And by all accounts he rose from the grave. That resurrection is one of the best-attested facts in history. It was the start of the Christian movement. Christianity got off the ground only because Jesus Christ rose from the dead. Christians all maintained then, and they have maintained ever since, that he is alive, and can be met and known by anyone anywhere. I am not at the moment asking you to believe it. I am simply asserting that this lies at the heart of Christianity. Christians believe that Jesus is alive.

With this fundamental conviction a lot of things change perspective. For one thing, death has its claws clipped. Jesus told his followers that they would join him after death. And when the author of those words backed them by actually rising from the grave, is it surprising that faith in the after-life with him should nerve Christians in the face of death and wipe away some of the tears from Christian mourners?

The relevance

That resurrection had other repercussions. Christianity rightly understood is not pie in the sky when you die. A lot of the pie is for now. And it consists not in having a good time but in enlisting in God's rescue operation for a world that is in a mess. The love and joy and peace and self-sacrifice of Jesus are qualities which he said he would pass on to his followers by means of his Spirit who would come to live in them. That he has done. And wherever you find authentic Christianity (there are plenty of imitations), you find something of the love and unselfishness and gaiety of Jesus. Believers do not write this world off and wait for the next. They get stuck in to problems of the illiterate, the sick, the inner city, the mentally disturbed. The social implications of the gospel are immense and far-reaching. The followers of Jesus are seeking in his strength to give an aroma of the kingdom of heaven through their lives and relationships and service here and now. They see themselves as the forerunners of the kingdom, a first instalment of the future crop. So there is a strong hope which nerves Christians on: the hope of exhibiting Christ's love and generosity here, then of being with him for ever. There is nothing selfish, or individualistic, narrow-minded or earthbound about Christianity. It is total response to the great God who has totally sacrificed himself out of love for us. When that begins to grip you, it makes big changes.

So it is not really a matter of which church you belong to, or whether to drink or not, or of singing hymns and looking prim. Christianity is a living relationship with Christ, God's Son, who loved us enough to die for us, and who is alive to give us his companionship, engage us in his enterprise, and give us his power. That is the claim. The question is, will it hold up? Is it true?

The truth?

This is a crucial question. Confucianism could survive even if it were proved beyond a shadow of doubt that Confucius never lived. It is his teaching that is important, not himself. The same is true, more or less, of all the great world religions (apart from Judaism and Christianity): history is not important to them. It is the ideas that matter.

But with Christianity history is important, and truth is important. For Christianity is not a system of beliefs or behaviour which could be maintained regardless of whether Christ lived or not. No, it is basically good news about a unique historical person; someone who was born a mere generation before the evangelists wrote, and was executed very publicly under the Roman prefect of Judea, Pontius Pilate. He claimed to embody God's self-disclosure to men. He backed that claim with his matchless teaching, his perfect life, and his well-attested resurrection.

That is the outline of the Christian story. There is nothing to be compared with it in the religions of the world. It has, indeed, features in common with the nature worship which underlay so many of the Eastern religions, based as this was on an annual cycle – the birth, maturity, death and resurrection of the year in its four seasons. The ancient Orient had many variations on this theme of death and resurrection in the cults of Dionysus, Attis, Isis and Osiris, Cybele and

Mithras. But with Christianity there was a fundamental difference. It was all attached to a historical person, a very special person, whom lots of people knew. It is all about the Jesus of history. Remove him from the centre of Christianity and there is nothing of substance left. Many of the ideals can be found elsewhere. Much of the ritual is universal coinage. But once disprove the historicity of Jesus Christ and Christianity will collapse like a pack of cards. And so it should. For Christianity claims that *these things happened*, that God was made manifest in our flesh, that he did die for us, that he is alive and relevant. And that is not a matter of ideology or mythology but of history. How well founded is this Christian claim? This is the question to which we turn in the next five chapters.

EVIDENCE

4

What is the secular evidence for Jesus?

This is an important question. An increasingly large propor-
tion of the human race, those under Marxist influence, are
being taught that Jesus Christ never lived. The Christian
story about a dying and a rising god was simply a variation
on a Near Eastern theme, invented by the early church to
compensate for their privations at the hands of the Roman
Empire. It is interesting to note that this view goes back to
Marx himself. It originated in the following way.

In 1842 a German theologian, Bruno Bauer, was deprived
of his university chair for heterodox opinions. This greatly
outraged Karl Marx, who not unnaturally thought he had
been cruelly wronged by the bourgeois men of religion: they
dared not allow the shaky foundations of their house of faith
to be investigated impartially. It was Bauer's view that the
historical Jesus was a figment of the imagination of the
evangelist Mark. It is one of the ironies of history, and a judgment on liberal Protestantism, that the vagaries of a heterodox theologian and the sharp reaction of the orthodox
should have laid the spiritual foundation for the most powerful atheistic regime the world has ever experienced.

What, then, is the evidence?

Testimony from Roman historians

One would not expect to find a lot of early secular evidence
about the existence of an obscure peasant teacher in an
unimportant province of the Roman Empire. Historians and

27

men of letters in the Empire were upper-class people who thoroughly disapproved of Eastern religions. Like Juvenal, they felt aggrieved that the Orontes had flowed into the Tiber, bringing a flood of decadent and very un-Roman cults in its wake. It would not be surprising if the humble birth of Christianity had gone entirely unnoticed by the historians of the period. But this is not so.

There are two famous references in the leading Roman writings of the period which put the power of the risen Lord and the historicity of Jesus beyond doubt. The fullest and most interesting comes in a letter from Pliny the Younger, governor of the province of Bithynia in Northern Turkey in the year AD 112. He wrote to tell the Emperor Trajan of the rapid spread of Christians in his province. It was becoming a major social problem. The pagan temples were closing down for lack of customers; the sacred festivals had been discontinued, and the demand for sacrificial animals had ceased. Clearly Christianity was very much on the move by the end of the first century, even in so remote a province as this on the edge of the Roman map. Pliny took the matter in hand. He executed those who persisted in their Christian faith; such people were obstinate, and deserved to die. But he confessed that he was unclear about the nature of their crime. He had discovered from those who recanted in the face of his persecution that no enormities were practised in the Christian meetings. Their whole guilt lay in this, that they refused to worship the imperial statue and the images of the gods, and were in the habit of meeting on a certain fixed day (*i.e.* Sunday) before it was light, when they sang a hymn to Christ as God (*quasi deo*). They took an oath (? the baptismal promise) not to commit crime. Their lives were exemplary, he conceded. You would not find fraud, adultery, theft or dishonesty among them. At their common meal they ate 'food of an ordinary and innocent kind'. (This is, no doubt, an allusion to the fact that Christians spoke of feeding on Christ in the Holy Communion: to the uninitiated this could look like cannibalism.) The whole thing was very perplexing to Pliny. That is why he consulted the Emperor. (*Letters*, 10.96.)

Cornelius Tacitus was a contemporary of Pliny. He was the greatest historian of Imperial Rome. He tells us how the Christians, hated by the populace for their 'crimes' (alluding no doubt to the Christian emphasis on 'love' which was given a sinister twist by the pagans and construed as incest), were made scapegoats for the Great Fire of AD 64 by the Emperor Nero. 'The name Christian', he writes, 'comes to them from Christ, who was executed in the reign of Tiberius by the procurator Pontius Pilate; and the pernicious cult, suppressed for a while, broke out afresh and spread not only through Judea, the source of the disease, but in Rome itself, where all the horrible and shameful things in the world collect and find a home.' (*Annals*, 15.44.)

It is clear that the patrician Tacitus has no sympathy for Christianity, practised as it was by the lowest classes. His evidence is therefore all the more valuable. He had good opportunity to get well informed about its origins, for in AD 112 he was governor of Asia, where Christians were numerous. Indeed, he referred to them again in a lost book of his *Histories*, of which an excerpt has been preserved in a later writer. In it Tacitus recognizes that Christianity began as a sect within Judaism, though by his own day it was quite distinct. And he gives the remarkable piece of information that the Roman general Titus hoped, by destroying the Temple at Jerusalem in AD 70, to put an end to both Judaism and Christianity, on the theory that if you cut the root, the plant will soon wither!

Curiously enough Pontius Pilate is not mentioned in any surviving pagan document other than this passage in Tacitus.[1] The one act for which he was remembered was the execution of Jesus Christ, who, as the Apostles' Creed puts it, 'suffered under Pontius Pilate'.

Writers of the stature of Pliny and Tacitus make the historicity of Jesus certain. But can we go back any further? Is there any first-century witness to Jesus among the pagan writers? It so happens that there is a little.

---

[1] Though Jewish writers speak of him, and an inscription to him has been found in Caesarea.

Additional attestation

To begin with, there is the statement by the Samaritan-born historian Thallus, who wrote in Rome about AD 52. His work is lost, but a fragment of it is preserved in the second-century writer Julius Africanus, who tells us, while discussing the darkness which fell when Jesus died on the cross (Mark 15:33), 'Thallus, in Book Three of his *History*, explains away the darkness as an eclipse of the sun – unreasonably as it seems to me.' Full marks to Julius Africanus for his objection! You cannot have a total eclipse of the sun when the moon is full, as it was at Passover when Jesus died. But the main interest of this quotation lies in showing that the circumstances of the death of Jesus were well known in Rome by the middle of the first century, and were thought significant enough by a non-Christian historian to be included in his history of the Eastern Mediterranean world from the Trojan War down to his own day!

There is a Syriac manuscript in the British Museum which contains a remarkable letter from Mara bar Serapion to his son. He writes from prison in the seventies of the first century, and reflects on the fate that is going to catch up with those who have persecuted a wise man like him!

> What advantage did the Athenians get from putting Socrates to death? Famine and plague came upon them as judgment for their crime. What advantage did the men of Samos get for burning Pythagoras? In a moment their land was covered with sand. What advantage did the Jews gain from executing their wise king? It was just after that their kingdom was abolished. God justly avenged these three wise men. The Athenians died of hunger. The Samians were overwhelmed by the sea. The Jews, ruined and driven from their land, live in complete dispersion. But Socrates did not die for good: he lived on in the teaching of Plato. Pythagoras did not die for good: he lived on in the statue of Hera. Nor did the wise king die for good: he lived on in the teaching which he had given. (B.M. Syriac MS 14658.)

Clearly the writer was not a Christian, or he would have said that Jesus lived on through rising from the dead. But he was influenced by Christians, and saw the destruction of Jerusalem as God's judgment for the execution of Jesus which they had procured.

It was not only the cross of Jesus, however, which was familiar to pagans in the fifties of the first century. So was the story of his resurrection, if we may judge by the probable significance of the following piece of evidence. A remarkable inscription has turned up, belonging to the reign of either Claudius (AD 41–54) or Tiberius (AD 14–38). In it the emperor expresses severe displeasure at reports he has heard of the removal of bodies of the dead from the tomb, and he gives warning that any further tampering with graves will incur nothing short of the death penalty. This inscription was found, significantly, at Nazareth, the home town of Jesus. This was clearly the imperial reaction to the report Pontius Pilate would inevitably have had to make on the execution of a political pretender (which is what Jesus would have appeared in Roman eyes). Emperors were very interested in such people! The early Christian writers knew that Pilate had in fact sent reports to the emperor about Jesus: for instance Justin Martyr, who wrote a *Defence* of Christianity about AD 150 and addressed it to the Emperor Antoninus Pius, said: 'That these things happened you may learn from the *Acts* which were recorded under Pontius Pilate', and again, 'That he performed these miracles you may easily satisfy yourself from the *Acts* of Pontius Pilate' (*1 Apology*, 35.7–9; 48.3). He also says that if anyone wanted to check on the registration of Joseph and Mary he would find evidence in those same *Acts* (*1 Apology*, 34.2: so Tertullian, *Against Marcion*, 4.7,19).

So it is pretty clear that Pilate had to report back on major incidents in his prefecture. He would presumably have taken the line alluded to in Matthew 28:11ff., that the disciples of Jesus came and stole the body while the soldiers who were supposed to be guarding the tomb slept. Highly embarrassing – though not as embarrassing as admitting to the resurrection! But we can well understand the sharpness of the imperial rejoinder.

31

There is another reference which has often been thought to refer to the emerging Christians. Suetonius, a court official under Hadrian and annalist of the imperial house, records that Claudius expelled the Jews from Rome because they were 'constantly making disturbances at the instigation of one Chrestus' (*Life of Claudius*, 25). The date was AD 49. Two of the people thus expelled were Aquila and Priscilla, who were Jews by birth but Christians by conviction (Acts 18:2). It appears that Suetonius thought Chrestus (or Christus – the pronunciation was indistinguishable then as in modern Greek) was the leader of one of the factions among the Jews. But clearly the disturbances were caused by the preaching of Christ among the large Jewish community of the capital, particularly as his supporters would urge that he was still very much alive. We have in this slightly muddled report the echo of the tremendous impact made by Christian preaching among the 10,000 or so Jews in Rome by the middle of the first century, and the acute division in the ghetto caused by the proclamation of a Jesus who was no myth but a very recent and very disturbing historical figure.

These major historians, Pliny (AD 61–114), Tacitus (AD 55–118?) and Suetonius (AD 69–140?), wrote of events which took place a mere thirty years before they were born. Moreover their official position gave them access to good historical information. The evidence they give is more than sufficient to establish the historicity of Jesus, the author of this new faith, who was executed under Pontius Pilate, prefect of the turbulent province of Judea from AD 26 to 36.

5
Is there any Jewish reference to Jesus?

It would not be surprising if no such evidence existed. We possess no Palestinian Jewish writings from the time of Jesus which might bear on the subject, and those which came from after the Fall of Jerusalem in AD 70 are inevitably influenced by the split between the church and the synagogue which had by then become irrevocable. Furthermore, the Jews felt that the Christians were responsible, at least in part, for the affairs leading up to the disastrous Jewish war. They resented the fact that the church had not helped them in the life-and-death struggle with Rome. And they were not best pleased at the meteoric rise of the new faith, which gained a lot of ground initially as a movement within Judaism.

So we shall not be surprised that there is little about Christ in the Jewish writings, and what there is is uncomplimentary.

Josephus

The most important witness is Josephus. He was one of the Jewish commanders in the war with Rome, and after AD 70 he set out to re-establish Jewish credit in the minds of Roman society. So he wrote his *Antiquities of the Jews* (AD 93) and his *Jewish War* (75–79) in order to inform the Roman public in the blandest way possible about the religion of his fathers. These apologetic works naturally kept to the minimum any material that would irritate their Roman readers. Nevertheless we meet in the pages of Josephus many of the

33

figures familiar from the New Testament: Pilate, Annas, Caiaphas, the Herods, Quirinius, Felix, Festus and many others. Josephus tells us about John the Baptist, his preaching, baptizing and execution. He gives James 'the brother of Jesus, the so-called Christ' a good write-up.

But most significant of all is his extended reference to Jesus himself:

> And there arose about this time [he means Pilate's time, AD 26–36] Jesus, a wise man, if it is right to call him a man, for he was a doer of marvellous deeds, a teacher of men who receive the truth with pleasure. He won over many Jews and also many Greeks. He was the Christ. And when Pilate had condemned him to the cross at the instigation of our own leaders, those who had loved him from the first did not forsake him. For he appeared to them alive again on the third day, as the holy prophets had foretold, and said many other wonderful things about him. And the race of Christians, so named from him, has not died out at this day (Josephus, *Antiquities* 18.3.3).

This is of course most surprising testimony to find in the pages of one who was certainly not a Christian. But no attempts to impugn its authenticity can be said to have succeeded. It has as good attestation as anything in Josephus; it is included in all the manuscripts. We know that the fourth-century historian Eusebius had it in his copy of Josephus. He quoted it twice. No doubt some of it is sarcastic: 'if it is right to call him a man' might be a snide allusion to his divine claims, or even be a Christian interpolation. 'He was the Christ' may refer to the charge affixed to his cross, while the passage about the resurrection may merely reflect Christian propaganda inserted later into the text. Even if the text has been touched up by some Christian editor (and there is no proof that it has), we have in this passage of Josephus a powerful, independent testimony to the historical reality of Jesus of Nazareth. The stories about Jesus were no myth. They were so circumstantial and so well-attested that they even found a place in this apologetic work of the Jewish

Josephus; and he had the strongest possible reasons for keeping quiet about anything so inconvenient for his theme.

The Mishnah

Unfortunately the Dead Sea Scrolls cannot help us. They were all written before Jesus was born. They shed a lot of light on the hopes and ideas of Essene Judaism in the century before Christ, but of course can tell us nothing about Jesus himself. For specific references we need to turn to the Mishnah (the Jewish Law Code) and the Talmuds (Commentaries on those Laws), which took shape after the Fall of Jerusalem in AD 70. Jesus is sometimes referred to as Jeshua ben Pantera, which may either reflect the Jewish libel that Jesus was the product of an illegitimate union between Mary and a Roman soldier Pantheras, or may be a corruption of the Greek word *parthenos* meaning 'virgin'. In either case it will refer to the birth of Jesus which was known to be unusual. The Jews knew all about the claim made for Jesus' birth from a virgin, and from the earliest days (when he was called 'the son of his mother' in Mark 6:3 – an unpardonable insult to a Jew), they put a sinister interpretation upon it. But even this provides some sort of confirmation for the Christian claim that Jesus' birth was *different*. Similar corroboration is found in the saying of Rabbi Eliezer:

> Balaam looked forth and saw that there was a man, born of a woman, who should rise up and seek to make himself God, and cause the whole world to go astray . . . Give heed that you go not after that man; for it is written, 'God is not man that he should lie' . . . And if he says that he is God, he is a liar, and he will deceive and say that he is departing and will come again at the End. He says it, but he will not perform it.

Such sentiments are characteristic of rabbinic opposition to Christianity. But consider what indirect attestation they afford to the Gospel story. Though Jesus is not referred to by name, it is plainly he who is meant by 'born of a woman' and

35

'seek to make himself God'. The divine claims of Jesus and his assertion that he would come again at the end of history are clearly reflected here, as is the recognition that Jesus' purposes embrace the whole world and not Jewry alone.

There are other passages which could be mentioned. One makes a biting pun on the word 'gospel'; another mentions Jesus' disciples; a third tells us that he performed miracles by means of magic which he learnt in Egypt (garbled allusions both to his miracles and to the flight into Egypt, recorded only in the Gospel of Matthew). Interestingly enough, Jewish sources never doubted the miracles of Jesus; but they attributed them to demonic agencies, as the Pharisees had done in the Gospels: 'by the prince of demons he casts out the demons' (Mark 3:22). Another passage records his execution: 'On the eve of Passover they hanged Jesus . . . because he practised sorcery and led Israel astray.'

Enough has been said to show that there are indeed Jewish allusions to Jesus, although there were strong reasons to keep quiet about him. They give some support for the historicity, unusual birth, miracles, teaching, disciples, Messianic claims, crucifixion, resurrection and promised return of Jesus, the author of the Christian faith. The Jewish evidence is well set out by a Jewish writer, Joseph Klausner, in *Jesus of Nazareth*, for those who want to examine the matter further. But it is clear that the Jewish evidence combined with the Roman in sketching at least the recognizable outlines of the Jesus who meets us in the Gospels. The fact that both Jewish and Roman authorities are strongly opposed to him makes their testimony all the more significant and valuable.

6

Does archaeology shed any light on the New Testament?

Archaeology can and does shed light on the New Testament in two main ways. There are some finds which help us to understand how the early Christians thought and believed. There are others which relate to the trustworthiness of the New Testament record.

Finds which shed light on Christian belief

There is a fascinating acrostic, which appears in several places as a Christian symbol, notably twice among the ruins of Pompeii, a city destroyed by the eruption of Vesuvius in AD 79. Christians (mentioned in inscriptions there) were present in Pompeii long before that date. Acrostics were as popular then as crosswords are now. This one was arranged in the shape of a square:

```
R O T A S
O P E R A
T E N E T
A R E P O
S A T O R
```

The straightforward meaning is unpromising: 'Arepo the sower holds the wheels with care (?).' But what is the hidden meaning which made it so congenial to the Christians? Here is the probable explanation.

In the first place, these letters add up to a repeated *Pater Noster* (the opening of the Lord's Prayer), with the addition of A and O twice:

```
                    A

                    P
                    A
                    T
                    E
                    R
  A PATERNOSTER O
                    O
                    S
                    T
                    E
                    R

                    O
```

The implications of this are tremendous. The address to God as Father stresses the unimaginable privilege felt by the early Christians in being adopted into his family through Jesus Christ. The cruciform shape emphasizes the centrality of the cross of Jesus, in itself as remarkable a thing as if a modern sect were to take the gallows as its badge. The repeated A and O (for Alpha and Omega, the first and last letters of the Greek alphabet) expresses Christian belief in the cosmic significance of Jesus. He is both the origin and goal of the universe.

The second feature in this remarkable acrostic which made it so acceptable to Christians seems to have been this. Where you have the A and O you have the T in between them. Now the Greek T was the emblem of the cross in the early church; for one thing it looked like one.[1] The placing of these Ts shows that Christians saw the cross of Jesus as the mid-point of history. That tells us how important history was to them. It tells us, too, the supreme significance in time and

[1] *The Epistle of Barnabas*, 9.8 makes great play with this symbolism.

eternity they saw in that cross, the very centre point between the A and O of the universe.

The crossword enthusiast will already have noticed that the repeated word TENET ('he holds') in the Rotas-Sator square also makes the shape of the cross. Is this accidental? Does it not rather betray a remarkable conviction? 'He holds', he sustains. In the midst of terrible persecution, when Christians were set ablaze as living torches to light up Nero's garden in AD 64, or when they were thrown alive to the lions in the Circus a little later, or were facing the flow of lava that engulfed Pompeii – *he holds!* No mythology, that. Their assurance was based on solid history, the history of Jesus, the A and O, who was executed in ghastly circumstances and yet rose triumphant. This was the ground for their confidence that the one who had conquered the grave could hold them, even in the jaws of death.

Another celebrated Christian symbol was the fish. It was used widely in the early church as an identification mark among Christians. It expresses very clearly and succinctly what they believed about Jesus. The Greek word for fish is *ichthus*, and each of the five Greek letters stands for a word: *Iesous Christos Theou Huios Soter*, 'Jesus Christ, Son of God, Saviour'. *Jesus*, a recent historical person. *Christ*, the long-awaited Messiah of the Jews, to whom all the prophets had borne witness and in whom the hopes of the nation reposed. *Son of God*, he was no mere man, but brought God into our humanity. And as *Saviour*, he rescues man from sin and death. That was a remarkably comprehensive creed, considering it had only five words in it! And notice how it underlines the fact that Christianity is Christ. It is entirely taken up with him.

A third fascinating piece of very early evidence must have a mention. The Israeli Professor Sukenik discovered in 1945 a sealed tomb just outside Jerusalem, in a suburb called Talpioth. It had escaped spoliation, and its contents were intact. There were five ossuaries, or bone caskets, in the tomb. The style of their decoration confirmed the indication of a coin found there that the tomb was closed in approximately AD 50. They are now on display in Jerusalem. On two of these ossuaries the name of Jesus appears clearly; one reads in Greek, *Iesu Iou* (?'Jesus, help') and the other in Aramaic, *Yeshu' Aloth* (?'Jesus, let him arise'). They are also marked with a cross.

Of course this find has caused controversy, but Sukenik's interpretation still seems probable that in these roughly scratched or charcoal inscriptions we have the earliest known allusion to Jesus by Christian believers. If so, the implications are remarkable. They point to a Jesus who is the Lord of life, who can bring help when a loved one has died. They point to Jesus as the risen Son of God who can raise the Christian dead to be with him. And all this within twenty years of the resurrection! It would be difficult to imagine any archaeological finds which could more clearly illustrate the burning faith of the early Christians in a Jesus whom many of them had known personally as a historical figure walking the streets of Palestine a few years previously.

Finds which shed light on New Testament testimony

Archaeology has also given us a great deal of light on the Gospels and Acts, again and again vindicating their reliability. Let us take a couple of examples from the Gospel of John, which used to be regarded by many critics as the latest and least historical of the Gospels. Chapter 5 tells of Jesus curing a paralysed man at the Pool of Bethesda. The evangelist remarks that it has five porticos. No sign of the pool had ever been found in Jerusalem. There was not even any mention of its name anywhere in Hebrew literature. It seemed that John was making it all up, perhaps suggesting that there was no healing to be had in the five porticos of the Jewish Law!

But a few years ago they found the Pool of Bethesda. It is one of the most interesting places in all Jerusalem, for beneath it lies an old pagan curative shrine dating from before the time when the Jews came to Palestine. No wonder there were rumours of strange powers in those waters! As John says, it has five porticos. They are remarkably well preserved. And the Copper Scroll found at Qumran gives an almost contemporary mention of the Pool of Bethesda. Both the name and the pool have turned up, and those who thought John was romancing got red faces.

Again, in chapter 19 John tells us that Jesus was tried at a place called The Pavement, or, in Hebrew, *Gabbatha* (19:13). Nobody knew anything of any such pavement. It looked like embroidery on the simple tale of Christ's trial, until the French archaeologist Père Vincent triumphantly dug it up in the 1930s. It is the most moving memorial of first-century Jerusalem to be seen in the holy city today. It measured fifty yards square, and seems to have been the pavement of the Roman barracks, situated near enough to the Temple to observe what went on and prevent riots. It was probably here that Jesus went on trial before Pilate. Buried under piles of rubble in the fall of Jerusalem in AD 70, it was not heard of again until its discovery a few decades ago. So John's tradition was seen to be no embroidery, but highly accurate information to which he could have had no access after AD 70.

There are many such instances where the accuracy of Luke has been vindicated. The writings of the classical archaeologist Sir William Ramsay, such as *Paul the Traveller and Roman Citizen* and *The Bearing of Recent Discovery on the Trustworthiness of the New Testament*, are particularly interesting on this subject. He began with the assumption that you could not believe a word Luke said unless it had independent testimony; but he was driven to the conclusion, the more he looked into it, that Luke was the best historian since Thucydides. It is interesting to see how modern Roman historians prize Luke's Gospel and Acts as accurate, reliable historical material for understanding the first-century world. He is amazingly accurate, for example, over the complicated nomenclature of local officials; he never puts a foot wrong. He knows that Thessalonica has 'politarchs' (Acts 17:6), Malta 'a first man' (28:7), Philippi two magistrates known as *strategoi* (16:20) and Ephesus a *grammateus* or 'recorder' (19:35). All of these have been confirmed by inscriptions. The scenes he paints of Athens, Corinth, Ephesus and the journey to Rome ring absolutely true in the ears of those best able to judge.

Perhaps the most amusing and significant turn-up for the

book is the case of Gallio. We are well informed about him, as it happens, for he was Seneca's brother. The details of his career were so well documented by Seneca, Tacitus and others that there did not seem room for a proconsulate in Greece which Luke accords him (Acts 18:12). There was much shaking of learned heads and mutterings about the unreliability of Luke, until an inscription was discovered which not only showed that Gallio was indeed proconsul of Achaea, but even gave us the year, AD 51. What was once thought to be a mark of Luke's fertile imagination has become the lynchpin of New Testament chronology!

It so happens that Corinth has proved particularly rich in finds which illuminate the New Testament record. For example, part of the door of the synagogue there has been unearthed with the inscription '. . . agogue of the Hebrews' clearly visible upon it. We can imagine Paul getting thrown out of there for preaching to the Gentiles, and setting up his assembly of Christians next door to the synagogue in the house of Titius Justus (Acts 18:7). Later he was brought to trial before Gallio: 'the Jews made a united attack upon Paul and brought him before the tribunal' (Acts 18:12). Well, that large stone tribunal has been dug up. And in 1929 a first-century marble slab was found at Corinth with this Latin inscription, 'Erastus, in consideration of his appointment as curator of buildings, laid this pavement at his own expense.' It is highly probable that we should identify this man with Paul's friend Erastus, the city treasurer of Corinth, from whom he sends greetings in Romans 16:23.

Of course, accuracy on details like these does not prove that the New Testament writers are necessarily reliable in the total picture of Jesus which they present. But if, where they can be tested, they come through with flying colours, does this not provide at least some initial presumption that they can be trusted where external confirmation is lacking?

7

How trustworthy is the
New Testament evidence for Jesus?

Granted that Jesus left some mark on the secular writers of his day, it is to the New Testament that we must turn if we want to know about his life, teaching and significance. Can we trust the picture the New Testament gives us? There are at least three sides to this question.

The reliability of the manuscript tradition

In the first place, have we got the New Testament substantially as it was written, or has it been tampered with in the succeeding centuries? This is a fascinating and important question: it is all too easy to evade the challenge of some part of the New Testament by saying, 'Well, that bit was probably put in later.'

But it so happens that we are in a much better position to judge the reliability of the manuscript tradition of the New Testament than we are with any other ancient book. The gap between Thucydides' writing of his *History* and the earliest manuscript we have of it is some 1,500 years. In the case of Tacitus it is 800 years. This does not unduly worry classical scholars. They do not doubt that the manuscript tradition is broadly reliable. Why, then, should anyone raise these doubts over the Christian documents? The answer lies, of course, in the issues at stake. The Christian material is so challenging and disturbing that it would be very convenient if we could write off the reliability of the text. But that is just what we cannot do.

In striking contrast to the handful of manuscripts we possess of the first-century classical authors, we have literally hundreds of the New Testament. They are written in a variety of languages, and they come from all over the ancient world. Although there are many variant readings in these manuscripts, it would be fair to say two things without the possibility of denial. The first is that no single point of Christian doctrine depends on a disputed reading. The second is that the text is so certain that anybody who attempted to make conjectural emendations (common when dealing with classical manuscripts) would be laughed out of court. Moreover our extant manuscripts are not separated by a great gap of hundreds of years from the originals. We have the four Gospels in papyrus books written before AD 200, little over a century after the originals. We actually have a fragment of the Gospel of John found in Upper Egypt, which experts date as early as AD 125. A document called *The Unknown Gospel* was discovered a generation ago, written before AD 150, which draws heavily on all four Gospels, thus showing the position they had already attained by that date. The early heretic Valentinus, whose *Gospel of Truth*, written about AD 130, has even more recently come to light, quoted the New Testament writings extensively: you need to quote the acknowledged stuff if, like Valentinus, you are keen to insert your own heresy! The church Fathers, Polycarp and Clement of Rome, writing thirty or forty years earlier than Valentinus, also quoted the New Testament extensively.

Thus by the end of the first century, that is to say within the lifetime of some who had known Jesus, the New Testament was not only written, it was on the way to being collected. And from the outset it was regarded as authoritative information about Jesus: so authoritative that Christians began to quote it with the same reverence that they accorded to the Old Testament. So authoritative that the heretics knew they must cite it extensively if they were to have a hope of taking in the faithful with their particular heresy. This all enabled Professor Kenyon, the celebrated biblical archaeologist, to conclude, 'The interval between the dates of the original composition and the earliest extant evidence becomes so small as to be negligible, and the last foundation for any doubt that the Scriptures have come down to us substantially as they were written has now been removed' (*The Bible and Archaeology*, p.288).

The reliability of the earliest New Testament witness

But granted we have the New Testament very much as it left its authors, can we believe them? Does not Paul, for example, transform the simple human Jesus of the Gospels into a divine Saviour after the pattern of Hellenistic myths? This is a hoary old chestnut, but it is worth looking into, because Paul's letters were completed before the Gospels and are in fact the oldest books in the New Testament. They are therefore of great importance.

Paul was a Roman citizen, a Jewish rabbi of great piety and learning, and a violent opponent of Christianity which he saw as a very dangerous heresy. How he was converted to the faith he had tried to destroy is a fascinating story in itself, and something, as Dr Johnson put it, 'to which infidelity has never been able to fabricate a specious answer'. But although he wrote independently of and prior to the four evangelists, his teaching about Jesus accords remarkably with theirs, especially when you remember that in his letters he is not setting out to inform his readers about Jesus. That had already been done when they were evangelized. He simply reminds them of various points that cropped up. Nevertheless we find him alluding to the divine pre-existence of Jesus,[1] his real humanity,[2] his obedience to the Law,[3] his life of loving service,[4] his teaching,[5] his institution of the Holy Communion,[6] and his death on the cross for man's forgiveness.[7] Paul can produce strong evidence of the resur-

[1] Colossians 1:15; 2:9; Philippians 2:6; *cf.* Mark 1:1; Matthew 1:23; 11:27; John 1:1.
[2] Galatians 4:4; Romans 1:4; *cf.* Luke 2:52; John 1:14; 4:6.
[3] Galatians 4:4; Matthew 5:17.
[4] 1 Corinthians 13; Galatians 2:20, and indeed the whole of the Gospels.
[5] 1 Corinthians 7:10; 9:14; *cf.* Mark 10:10f.; Luke 10:7.
[6] 1 Corinthians 11:23; *cf.* Mark 14:22ff.
[7] Romans 3:24; 2 Corinthians 5:19–21; *cf.* Mark 10:45.

rection, of which the Gospels make so much. He tells us in 1 Corinthians 15 of James, the unbelieving brother of Jesus who became a Christian because of the resurrection; of Peter, who was convinced by it and became the cornerstone of the Christian mission; of his own astonishing conversion on the Damascus Road, and of the 'five hundred brethren at once' who saw Christ after his resurrection. Some of these, he tells us, had died by the time he wrote the letter to Corinth, in AD 53. But most of them were still alive, and would be glad to substantiate the resurrection claims!

In this very same passage Paul refers to the oldest written material in Christendom. It was a very early creed which he had passed on to the Corinthians. Its clauses are all marked by the word *that*.

> For I delivered to you as of first importance what I also received,
> *that* Christ died for our sins in accordance with the scriptures,
> *that* he was buried,
> *that* he was raised on the third day in accordance with the scriptures,
> and *that* he appeared to Cephas, then to the twelve . . .
> (1 Corinthians 15:3–5).

Those four *thats* enshrine a precious kernel of Christian belief from the very earliest days of the church. Paul reminds the Corinthians that he had told them all this when he evangelized them, in AD 49. But it was much older than that. He tells us he had received it when he was converted, which was at least fifteen years earlier (see Galatians 1:18; 2:1). We are getting back perilously close to the resurrection itself if we are forced to place Paul's conversion somewhere in the mid 30s AD.

But Paul still has not finished. In the words *I delivered . . . I received* he is using the language of received tradition and its transmission. In other words, the resurrection creed he cites here was already *traditional* in Christian circles before he became a Christian. It takes us back to the very first days of the church.

There is not much chance for myth and embellishment to have crept in here. And there is no conflict between the teachings of Paul and of the earliest Jerusalem church: 'Whether then it was I or·they, so we preach and so you believed' (1 Corinthians 15:11). That is why Professor A. M. Hunter can write, after examining the subject with great care:

The charge of Paul being the great innovator or corrupter of the gospel must be dropped for good and all. Original Paul certainly was, but the thing about which he wrote with such originality and creative power was not his own discovery or invention . . . He took it over from those who were in Christ before him. Is not this a conclusion of quite capital importance? (*Paul and his Predecessors*, p.150.)

It is indeed. There are very few ancient events on which we have such strong, early and united testimony.

The reliability of the Gospels

What are we to make of the Gospels themselves? The great thing to remember is that they are an entirely new literary *genre*. Clearly, they are not biographies of Jesus in the conventional sense. What biography would fail to tell us of any of the physical features or personal details of its hero, pass over thirty of his thirty-three (?) years without mention, and concentrate up to half of its account on his death?

Equally obviously, they are not histories either, in the normally accepted sense of the word. The evangelists cheerfully bring God and his actions into the story – which would look odd in a history book. On the whole they are singularly lacking both in chronology and in references to what is going on in the secular world.

The Gospels are basically the proclamation of good news: good news about Jesus, who, the writers have come to believe, is God's way of rescue for men.

This explains why the Christians did not write down their Gospels for some thirty or forty years after the events they record. They were so busy preaching this good news that they did not bother to put pen to paper. Writing was a laborious and expensive process before the days of the printing press, and was not valued in antiquity nearly as much as the spoken word. So for thirty years and more the Christian message was carried by word of mouth, until the eyewitnesses began to die off, and it became imperative to preserve their testimony for succeeding generations. It was then that the Gospels were compiled, between the seventh and ninth decade of the first century (the actual dates are much in dispute).

But if they were written down so late, surely they are unreliable? In one of the most influential Christian books to be written this century, *The Apostolic Preaching and its Developments,* Professor C. H. Dodd showed that much the same pattern of preaching about Jesus can be found in all the independent strands that go to make up the New Testament. There can be little doubt that such unplanned homogeneity faithfully represents the original Christian message.

We can in any case verify some of what the evangelists record. Thus, for example, the survival of eyewitnesses to the time when the Gospels were written down is a considerable control on their truthfulness. Again, the absence in the Gospels of major concerns of the early church is a notable point in favour of their truthfulness. If the church had cooked up the contents of the Gospels, we would have expected them to have put into Jesus' mouth matters which were of burning concern to themselves. But on the contrary we find that these issues (the Lordship of Jesus, the Holy Spirit, the circumcision controversy, the Jewish-Gentile split and meat offered to idols) are conspicuous by their absence.

Or take the parables. Do these go back to Jesus himself? Assuredly. Why should anyone have pretended that Jesus taught in this remarkable way if he did not? Who could have been the genius to make them up, if not he? One thing is clear. Nobody in Judaism before him taught in parables like that. And nobody after him was able to continue it. The early church did not teach in parables: but they knew Jesus had done so.

Two useful criteria

Let us apply two tests to the teaching of Jesus. They are much valued by theologians. One is the principle of multiple attestation. If something is attested in more than one strand of the Gospel material, there is strong ground to argue its authenticity. Well, apply that to something even as improbable as the feeding of the five thousand. In the Gospels there are no less than four accounts of this feeding by Jesus out of next to no materials. How much more attestation are we going to need before we will credit it?

The other test is the matter of Aramaic. The Aramaic experts have shown that a good deal of the teaching of Jesus goes back very easily into Aramaic, his native tongue in which presumably he generally taught. What is more, when that has been done, it falls into a poetic and memorable form. Is this why the retentive Eastern memory was able to remember it with such precision over the years and enshrine it in our Gospels? Scandinavian New Testament scholars like H. Riesenfeld and B. Gerhardsson have argued forcibly that Jesus formally instructed his disciples by heart, in some parts of his teaching, as the Jewish rabbis did. They maintain, moreover, that this teaching was conceived of as 'holy word', to be transmitted carefully to others. This could account for many of the similarities, even to word formation and order, in the Gospel stories. Whether or not their theory holds, they have drawn attention to the essential Jewishness of the Gospels: and Jews learnt by memorizing.

Gospel criticism is complicated and specialized. This is not the place to go further into it. But we can be confident that there is no question of Christians being on the run about their foundation documents. These books which go to make up our New Testament have been subjected to a degree of scrutiny and criticism, by opponents and friends of the Christian faith alike, which has been given to no other documents in history – and that includes Shakespeare! After all that, the standing of the Gospels is as high as ever. No, it is not the Christians who are wearing blinkers about the Gospels. It is those who have not read them for a long time (if at all) who

may well be evading the issue. They have a horrible sus-
picion that if they expose themselves to the primary
evidence in this way they may be convinced – and that would
be inconvenient.

8
Did Jesus rise from the dead?

The heart of the matter

The heart of the matter lies not in the precise accuracy of every detail in the Gospels, but in the resurrection of Jesus Christ from the dead. That is what sparked the Christian movement into existence. That is why people were persuaded that he was the Son of God. These words of Paul in Romans (1:3f.) look like an early creed he is quoting: 'the gospel of his Son, who was descended from David according to the flesh and designated Son of God in power . . . by his resurrection from the dead, Jesus Christ our Lord.' He was one of us all right: descended from David. He was Son of God, no less: and he showed it by his resurrection from the dead.

That is the Christian claim. And they got it from Jesus himself. In one debate with the scribes they ask him for a sign of who he is – as if they had no signs to go on! So Jesus refuses to give them a compulsive sign. He does not want reluctant conscripts among his followers. Instead, he points them to the crux of whether he is or is not what he claims to be: the resurrection would be the touchstone of truth.

'An evil and adulterous generation seeks for a sign,' said he; 'but no sign shall be given to it except the sign of the prophet Jonah. For as Jonah was three days and three nights in the belly of the great fish, so will the Son of man be three days and three nights in the heart of the earth' (Matthew 12:39f.).

51

If you really want to get to the heart of Christianity, it is to the resurrection you must turn. Look at it hard and critically, but with an open mind. For this is an area where it is all too easy to be blinded by our presuppositions and prejudices; and that applies to Christians and to non-Christians alike. If the resurrection did not happen, then it is high time I gave up being a Christian. I am deluded. But if it did take place, the implications are enormous, and it is no good running away from them. It means Jesus is indeed the Son of God. It means he is *the* way to God, and we need not waste our time and effort looking into every religion from Jainism to Yoga, via Zen and Krishna. It means the cross was not the end, and the atonement for human sins which he there achieved is effective for any who will have it. It means that there is a life after death, and you and I had better take that into account. It means, on a broader canvas, that there is hope for our world. It means, too, so Paul told the Athenians, that in the resurrection we have a firm pointer to the fact that God will one day judge us; and ignorance on that day will be no excuse. 'The times of ignorance God overlooked, but now he commands all men everywhere to repent, because he has fixed a day on which he will judge the world in righteousness by a man whom he has appointed, and of this he has given assurance to all men by raising him from the dead' (Acts 17:30f.).

Examine the facts

Let us begin by taking off our dark glasses. We all tend to wear them. The Christians say, 'He must have risen, because it is in the Bible, or in the tradition of the church.' The sceptics say, 'He couldn't have risen, because dead men don't.' Both sides must be open to the evidence. It is no good Christians kidding themselves that Jesus rose if he did not. It is no good sceptics saying it could not have happened if it did. Dead men are indeed not in the habit of leaving their tombs. But any dead men we know have all succumbed to the human disease of sin and failure. We do not know what would happen when a perfect specimen of mankind died.

52

There have not been any until and apart from Jesus Christ. We are simply not in a position to say that he could not have broken the bands of death. So we had better examine the evidence.

The evidence is very strong. So strong that, although attempts have been made to crack it ever since the first century, no single alternative explanation has ever survived for long. They simply do not bear critical investigation. If you are interested in following this up, you could see what a leading lawyer thinks about it in Sir Norman Anderson's *The Evidence for the Resurrection*; or an archbishop in A. M. Ramsey, *The Resurrection of Christ*; or a journalist in Frank Morison, *Who Moved the Stone?* There is not space to go into this here in any detail. I have tried to do so in *The Day Death Died*. But the essence of the case can be laid out very simply.

The first thing to be very clear about is that Jesus was dead. This would hardly be worth saying (survivors of crucifixion being rather scarce!) were it not for theories that Jesus revived in the cool of the tomb and walked out into the Easter sunshine. Jesus was very dead on Good Friday evening. He was certified as such by the experienced execution squad and their commanding officer, the centurion. Pilate recognized he was dead, before allowing his body to be removed: political agitators were dangerous commodities with fidgety Roman emperors getting worried about competition. But just to make sure, we are told that the soldiers were noticed sticking a spear into his side. And the eyewitness who records this says 'blood and water' came out (John 19:34). He could not have known that he was bearing testimony to the strongest possible indication of death: the separation of blood into clot and serum. Had Jesus still been alive, bright spurts of arterial blood would have emerged from the wound. Jesus was unquestionably dead.

What happened next? There are four strands of evidence which, taken together, point unmistakably in one direction. Here they are. Reflect on them.

Consider the beginnings of the Christian church

It began at Easter, three days after the disciples of Jesus had been crestfallen and scattered. The leader from whom they hoped so much had been strung up like a common criminal and had met an untimely and disgraceful end. Something turned these dispirited people into a force which rocked the Roman empire. They were perfectly clear what it was. 'This Jesus, whom you crucified, God raised up, and of that we all are witnesses' (Acts 2:32). And when you recall that the church had nothing distinctive about it apart from the belief in Jesus' resurrection, you see what a powerful argument this is. In all other respects they were orthodox Jews. But they simply had to start a new movement because of the unthinkable revolution that had occurred. There had never been anything like it in history. A perfect life, lofty claims, matchless teaching, a martyr's death, and all that crowned by resurrection.

The church had three things about it from the very start which underlined the conviction that Jesus was alive. First, there was Sunday, called 'the Lord's day' in the New Testament (Revelation 1:10). It was their day of rest and celebration. It was called the Lord's day because that was the day, the first day of the week by Jewish reckoning (Mark 16:2), on which Jesus rose from the grave. As Jews they would have had the strongest reasons to abide by the time-honoured sabbath. Look how jealously Jews guard it today. Well, *these men changed the day of rest!* They reckoned that it was even more important to celebrate the new creation when Jesus rose from the dead than it was to recall the old creation when God made the world. Something amazing is required to have brought about that change. The Gospels tell us what it was – the resurrection.

Not only the day of rest, but the Christian sacraments are inextricably intertwined with the resurrection. What is baptism but a symbolic entering into the dying and rising of Jesus (Romans 6:3ff.)? It is a death to the old life and a new beginning with the risen Jesus. That is what it means. They would never have invented a sacrament like that if the resurrection had not been the very centre of their convictions. It was the same with the Lord's Supper. This sacrament which Jesus left to his disciples was no mere remembering of a dead Jesus. It was a meal with the living Jesus. That is why we read that they broke bread 'with exultation' (Acts 2:46). They were partaking in table fellowship with their risen and ascended Lord. They were tasting the first-fruits of the Messianic banquet in heaven. Neither of these two Christian sacraments would have been thinkable if the disciples had not been convinced that Jesus had risen from the grave.

Consider the empty grave of Jesus

Everyone is agreed that the tomb of Jesus was empty on the first Easter Day. Had this not been the case, the Jews could very easily have silenced the infant church when it began to preach the resurrection. They would have said, 'What non-sense! His tomb is around the corner, and his body is rotting in it. We will prove it to you: come and see.' They would have loved to say something like this. It would have avoided a lot of embarrassment and would have nipped the new move-ment in the bud. But they were not able to say anything of the sort. Incidentally, the fact that they could not produce the body shows that the Jews had not moved it. Not that they would have wanted to: they were only too pleased to have got him dead and buried at last. Equally the Romans did not move the body of Jesus. They, too, wanted a quiet life and would not have done anything so stupid. If by any chance they had, they would have been able to point to the correct tomb with its decomposing occupant when the disciples began six weeks later to disturb the peace, from the Day of Pentecost onwards, with large open-air meetings in the streets which led to major riots.

This really leaves open only the possibility that the dis-ciples robbed the grave. But is this credible? Could they have got through the guard posted on the tomb by the Jews (Matthew 27:65; 28:11f.)? And would they? After all, they were prepared to be laughed at, had up before the leaders of their nation, imprisoned, whipped, torn limb from limb, and turned into human torches for this conviction that Jesus was alive. Would they have endured that for a fraud? How are we to account for the note of discovery and unselfconscious joy that runs through the pages of the New Testament, and particularly the account of the growth and spread of the church in Acts, if the whole thing is based on a fraud? No, that will not do. I am not aware of any unprejudiced person who has gone into the evidence carefully and emerged with the belief that this explanation will hold water. Very well then, if the body of Jesus was not removed by his friends or his enemies, that leaves only one possibility. It is that God raised him from the dead to a new quality of life on the first Easter Day, just as the astonished and joyful Christians maintained.

Consider the appearances of Jesus

He did not leave us with an empty tomb alone. That by itself would scarcely have persuaded hard-boiled fishermen and tax collectors that he was alive. He appeared to them, not once but many times, over a period of six weeks. And then it ended, and from the Day of Pentecost onwards he has been encountered by Christian believers in a different way, by his Spirit being released to enter our lives. The resurrection appearances were designed to prepare the disciples for this, to assure them that he was indeed Lord of the grave and was from now on to be known in a different way.

These appearances have all the marks of authenticity. The first ones were to women, which no Jew would have fabricated were it not true: women were disqualified from giving evidence in Judaism! And all the accounts show an initial disbelief in the disciples; like Thomas, who wanted to put his fingers into the nail-holes in Jesus' hand before totally committing himself, the disciples had no desire to succumb to fairy-tales. Any suggestion that these appearances were hallucinations would be very hard to support. These appearances happened to different groups, in different places, at different times. That is most uncharacteristic of a hallucination. On one occasion Jesus appeared to more than 500 people at one time. Were they all hallucinated? Consider the resurrection appearances, and see if you can come up with an alternative explanation that really carries conviction.

Consider the lives changed by the resurrection

We have already looked at the very early evidence of 1 Corinthians 15:5–8 on the resurrection of Jesus. The list, as we have seen, was traditional in Christian circles before the conversion of Paul in the mid-thirties. It tells of some of the lives that were changed by the resurrection of the dead, and it does so by using a remarkable tense. In Greek, the aorist tense is normally used to indicate a past event: they used the perfect to show a past event whose effects continue. Now when recording the events which brought Christianity into being, Paul uses the aorist: 'Christ died' . . . 'was buried' . . . 'appeared' are all aorists. But when he wants to remind them that Jesus rose, the aorist will not do for him. Breaking the sequence of tenses he throws in a perfect: *egegertai!* This means 'he rose and is alive' (1 Corinthians 15:4). That is what accounts for the changes in the lives of the men, he adduces. The fact that Jesus not only rose but is still alive changed everything for these his contemporaries: and it has been doing so ever since.

'He appeared to Cephas', who was changed by that en-counter from a coward and a turncoat to a man of rock on whose courage and witness the early church was founded. Just sense the resurrection joy bursting from him: 'Blessed be the God and Father of our Lord Jesus Christ! By his great mercy we have been born anew to a living hope through the resurrection of Jesus Christ from the dead' (1 Peter 1:3).

'Then to the twelve', says Paul. The twelve, who had for-saken Jesus at his hour of crisis, are now to be found stand-ing up for him boldly in synagogue, Sanhedrin and open air, in prison and in courtroom. Quite a change! And it was the resurrection that did it.

'Then he appeared to more than five hundred brethren at one time, most of whom are still alive, though some have fallen asleep.' The five hundred, presumably followers of

Jesus in Galilee, were changed by that resurrection from a rabble into a church: humble, joyful and confident.

'Then he appeared to James.' That was quite something. James was his brother, and his brothers thought that Jesus was mad and did not believe in him while he was alive (Mark 3:21; John 7:5). But we find that they became leaders in the early church. James and Jude have both left letters in the New Testament, and James was leader of the Jerusalem church. How come? It was the resurrection that did it. He appeared to James.

'Then to all the apostles' – presumably an allusion to Thomas who had not been with them the first time Jesus had appeared, and was determined not to believe. But meeting the risen Christ drew from him the strongest confession of faith to be found anywhere in the New Testament: 'My Lord and my God!' (John 20:24–31).

'Last of all, as to one untimely born, he appeared also to me,' says Paul. Everybody knows about that Damascus Road experience. It changed the most determined enemy of Christ into his most dedicated apostle and martyr.

When you consider honestly and soberly the change in the lives of these men, and of millions since all over the world, of every background and nationality and culture; when you consider that they all put it down to the resurrection; when you reflect on the remarkable fact that they do not simply claim that he rose, but that he lives and that they know him and communicate with him – then I think you will agree that we have very strong evidence that resurrection did take place and that the risen Christ is a force to be reckoned with today.

Good news

I received recently a letter from someone who had been helped to faith by my book on the resurrection, *The Day Death Died*:

Your book has opened the eyes of the most doubting Thomas there ever was. Thank you for writing so clearly about the resurrection. I had known about it since child-hood, but the penny has only just dropped, and I'm nearly fifty.

Why, oh why, isn't the resurrection *shouted* out in our churches every Sunday? This is the good news I've been looking for for so long. I had always thought the good news was the forgiveness of sins – and it didn't make much sense and certainly I wasn't very grateful. This is far, far more!

It is indeed. It is the best news ever brought to mankind. It is the very heart of Christianity.

9
The evidence - so what?

In the old days, if the evidence pointed in a certain direction, you would expect people to move in that direction. But not today. For many people there has grown a great gulf between evidence and action. We do not act on reason alone, as we fondly suppose: but on prejudice, on impulse, or on emotion. Of course (especially if we are males) we like to rationalize our actions! But that must not conceal from us the fact that our decisions are often arrived at through routes other than the reason.

So it is worth pausing for a moment to draw out the implication of the evidence we have been looking at so far. We have seen that there is good reason to suppose that Christianity is no illusion, no mere crutch for the mentally and emotionally crippled. We have seen that there is good reason to regard the Gospels as trustworthy accounts of the life and teachings and death of Jesus, written by disciples and contemporaries. We have seen that there is external evidence in non-Christian sources to support the picture we derive of Jesus from the New Testament. And we have seen that it is very much harder to argue against his resurrection than it is to argue for it. So what?

We cannot leave it there. To do so is intellectual and moral cowardice.

Evidence demands action.

Evidence demands commitment

Evidence by itself can never change us. Evidence about Jesus by itself can never make us into Christians. We have to do something about it. There is a lovely piece in Kierkegaard's book *Philosophical Fragments* where he observes that even if you had been able to keep as close to Jesus as the pilot fish to the shark, so that you did not miss anything he did or said, that would not make you a disciple. He was perfectly correct. You would need to commit yourself on the basis of that evidence before you became a disciple. There is in Christian belief an intellectual and a volitional side. We need to be clear on the evidence; and then we need to commit ourselves to it wherever it leads.

The writers of the New Testament were honest people of varied background who had all come to believe in Jesus, and wrote to explain why they had done so. Their evidence does not compel belief, in the sense of commitment. The evidence linking smoking with lung cancer is indisputable, yet there are plenty of people who choose to shut their eyes to it and go on smoking. But that is not the fault of the evidence. Evidence can never induce people to believe. It can, how- ever, offer reasonable grounds for belief. That is what the New Testament affords – reasonable grounds for belief. Nobody is forced to act on it. Pontius Pilate and the Pharisees did not commit themselves to the Christian cause, and they were not short of evidence: they decided to steer clear. Similarly, there are plenty of able and intelligent people in our own day who do not believe. This, however, is not because the evidence is insufficient to warrant belief. It is usually either because they have not examined it personally, or else because they are unwilling to commit themselves to the challenge of Christian living. Let me give you a well- known example of each of those positions.

Reject it . . . ?

The first is Bertrand Russell. He was a highly intelligent atheist who apparently had not given much attention to the evidence provided by the New Testament. To judge from his essay in *Why I am not a Christian* he can have given only a cursory glance at what the New Testament actually says, or he would not be able to make such astonishingly naïve comments about Christianity. When I first read that essay I expected a powerful intellectual attack on Christianity, because I had studied philosophy and had been deeply impressed by his brilliance. But I was disappointed. I found he did not even begin to examine two of the most powerful planks in the Christian position, the claims of Jesus and his resurrection from the dead. He simply did not attempt to come to terms with the New Testament evidence. And for a man of Russell's ability that is decidedly unimpressive. He preferred to evade Jesus by taking refuge in generalities.

Aldous Huxley represents the other type of atheist. He admits with delightful candour that he was unwilling to commit himself to the demands of Christian discipleship. In a fascinating passage in *Ends and Means* he writes:

> I had motives for not wanting the world to have a meaning; consequently assumed that it had none, and was able without any difficulty to find satisfying reasons for this assumption. The philosopher who finds no meaning in the world is not concerned exclusively with a problem in pure metaphysics. He is also concerned to prove that there is no valid reason why he personally should not do as he wants to, or why his friends should not seize political power and govern in the way that they find most advantageous to themselves ... For myself, the philosophy of meaninglessness was essentially an instrument of liberation, sexual and political. (*Ends and Means*, pp.270 f.)

It is not often that one gets as honest an admission of running away from the truth as that.

... Or follow it?

The evidence for the Christian cause is very strong. Though incapable of compelling faith, it is more than sufficient to warrant it. For faith is *self-commitment on evidence*. And the New Testament gives us the evidence on which we are challenged to commit ourselves. So it seemed to those first Christians, Jews to a man. Stark monotheists as they were, schooled in centuries of faith in one God, they nevertheless found themselves impelled by the facts which they record in the New Testament to believe in and commit themselves to Jesus. Slowly they came to the conclusion that this Jesus was not simply a man, but God almighty accommodating himself to human nature and living in their midst. The Gospels give us their testimony to what they found Jesus to be: they also furnish us with evidence on which we are called to decide.

A great many people who are inclined to dismiss Christians as escapists have never personally examined the grounds for the Christian claims. This struck J. B. Phillips forcibly. In *Ring of Truth* he wrote:

Over the years I have had hundreds of conversations with people, many of them of a higher intellectual calibre than my own, who quite obviously had no idea of what Christianity is really about . . . This I find pathetic and somewhat horrifying. It means that the most important event in human history is politely and quietly bypassed. For it is not as though the evidence had been examined and found unconvincing; it has simply never been examined.

A great many people who would consider themselves well educated have never (at least since growing up) read through the New Testament, and particularly the Gospels, with an open mind. Others stay on the run because they would not be willing to commit themselves to Christ even if they were persuaded intellectually by what they read in the New Testament. But there is no point in asking for evidence if we are going to cry 'so what?' when it is presented to us. We then need the moral courage to follow where it leads.

This is what happened to E. V. Rieu some years ago. He was an agnostic classical professor, and he had to study the Gospels carefully while writing the Penguin translation. He saw where the evidence pointed. He had the courage to take the appropriate action, and it led him to Christian discipleship.

I remember a research scientist once saying to me that he thought the story of Jesus was mythical. I asked him when he had last read it. He had to admit that it was a long time ago. I said to him something like this. 'You are a scientist. You are accustomed to modifying your preconceived theories if the evidence warrants it. I suggest that you apply the same principle here. Examine the evidence for yourself. Be open to where it may lead you. Just follow the truth, and see what happens.' He did. I next met that man some months later in a Christian meeting. 'I did what you suggested', he said, 'and it has brought me into the Christian camp.'

His example is not a bad one to follow if you have thought hitherto that it is the Christians who are on the run. At least it will show you are not.

OBJECTIONS

10
Is the agnostic account of man satisfying?

In the next four chapters I want to look at four common propositions. They are put forward in good faith, often enough. But I believe them to be escapist. They are all objections to the Christian faith, and they run something like this.

'I'm a humanist. I believe in doing good, like you lot.'

'In a scientific age you've got to give up believing in Christianity.'

'Christianity is irrelevant these days.'

'Christianity? Too dull for me.'

These all purport to be reasons for leaving Christ out of our life: I believe them to be excuses.

Christian humanism

A lot of people call themselves humanists these days. Christians should, too: it would clarify the thinking. For humanism in Western Europe began with the Christians. At the dawn of the Renaissance people such as Erasmus, Colet and More emerged. They were humanists. They strove for human enlightenment by allowing the Bible to speak for itself in reaction to the way in which people's spirits were fettered and their free enquiry after truth prevented in the Middle Ages. The Reformers, like Luther and Calvin, Bucer and Melanchthon, were strong on the rights of man. They were at one and the same time leading European intellectuals, churchmen and humanists! Confusion has arisen because atheistic humanism, which emphasizes that man is the centre of all things, has usurped the title and debased its meaning. But this strong strain of Christian humanism has continued to our own day. If you love God, it is hardly surprising that you will love your neighbour, too. Nor is it surprising that Christian humanists have been in the van of human progress – the freeing of slaves, the forming of trades unions, the banning of child labour and so forth. Education, medicine, care for the blind and the disabled – all these things were the fruit of Christian humanism.

A truly Christian humanism makes room both for hope and for realism about man and his world. Hope because the Christian believes in God, Creator, Saviour, Indweller. This God cared for us enough to become one of us: he will not scrap our world. There is room for optimism, if you believe in God. Equally the Christian humanist is a realist, well aware, as his scriptures no less than his observation tell him, of fallen human nature. He wears no rose-tinted spectacles about the goodness of mankind, and the virtues of either the aristocracy or the proletariat. He knows that, left to themselves, people are incurably selfish. The cross reminds him of what human wickedness is capable of. The resurrection reminds him of how God can overrule it.

Christian humanism makes sense. God holds the key to what being human is all about. Man is wonderful, but he is not almighty, nor sinless. Man is a temple, but a ruined temple. Man is intended to obey his Maker whose vice-regent he is on this earth. He honours and cares for his fellow men because they are precious: they are made in the image of God.

Atheistic humanism

But what happens when your humanism drops God out of the picture? You can still have the ideal of loving your fellows; but you might just as well liquidate them, if you can get away with it. Why not? There is no God, no judgment, no after-life, no ultimate standards. Why not, if you can get away with it? If you drop God out of the picture, other people are just biological accidents, like you. Why should you really bother about their welfare, so long as yours is secure? Do I hear you mutter something about innate generosity, unselfishness and love? Aren't those rather remarkable things to find in a naked ape, a chemical synthesis like man?

'Don't go into all that,' you say. 'I care about other people. I love them. Isn't that enough?' Well, it is certainly a great deal. And it is of the utmost importance. Christians have always paid lip-service to it, because it lies at the heart of the life and teaching of Jesus. Alas, we Christians have not always lived up to it. And we have reason to be ashamed of the many blotches which have disfigured Christian history, and still do. Jesus taught that the greatest thing in all the world was to love the Lord your God and your neighbour as yourself. So, leaving out for a moment the bit about loving God, the Christian and the non-Christian humanist are absolutely at one on practical policies. They are to love their neighbours as themselves.

But Christians will want to ask their non-Christian humanist friends three questions about love. Why, in their view, should we bother to love? What is it, anyhow? And how are we going to achieve it?

Why bother with love?

After all, it is demanding to put ourselves out for other people. Why should we take the trouble? Does that seem a stupid question? Is it not self-evident that in this global village we should do to others as we would like them to do to us? Well, it may be self-evident, but that doesn't mean people do it. It is self-evident to many folk that fidelity in marriage to one partner for life is the ideal: but somehow they don't get round to doing it. It is too demanding, too difficult. There has to be a very powerful motivation to shift us into costly self-sacrificing action. If you meet members of your government I have no doubt you will think them charming, generous people – well, perhaps with the odd exception. But set those people down with third-world leaders to work out a trade agreement that offers a fair reward for primary producers, and then you will see that there is not sufficient motivation for justice, let alone love. Maybe I should love my neighbour as myself, but somehow I don't get round to it, especially if he is out of sight and therefore out of mind.

This world is in desperate need of love. The pundits reckon that the nuclear clock is at four minutes to midnight. They tell us that the nuclear arsenals of the world contain one and a quarter million times the bomb-power that flattened Hiroshima. They assure us that every major city in the Northern hemisphere has been targeted for bombs two thousand times more powerful than that which fell on the Japanese city. They tell us that within the next ten years some fifty more countries will have the capability of making nuclear bombs if they so desire. And they *will* so desire, because Big Brother has got nuclear arms! Was there ever such a need for love in this small world? But where is it coming from? The facts I have just set down are well known, but who is doing anything much about them? There is just insufficient motivation in unchanged, unaided human nature to love and love and go on loving.

Well, you may say, what has Christianity to offer? A very simple but profound motive. 'We love, because he first loved us' (1 John 4:19). That is why. We see others made in God's image. Therefore it cannot be right to scrap them or neglect them. And we have a marvellous example in reaching out to the unlovely: that is what Jesus Christ did to us. We believe that love is at the heart of the universe; that God is love; and that he has loved us and lavished his care on us. That does something to you. That makes you stand high. That makes you want to go on loving others with the love that he has poured into you. The Christian imperative 'love your neighbour as yourself' is firmly grounded in the Christian indicative, 'the Son of God loved me and gave himself for me.' That is why bother!

What exactly is love?

The word has got devalued. What does it mean? Particularly what does it amount to on atheistic presuppositions? In an

68

impersonal and mechanistic world, all talk of love and morality is rather meaningless. I am reminded of Steve Turner's poem 'The Conclusion'.

> My love
> > she said
> > that when all's considered
> > we're only machines.
>
> I chained her to my
> > bedroom wall for future use,
> > and she cried.

In a world that had no creator and is going nowhere there can be no absolutes. Not even love or goodness. All is relative. We all do our own thing . . .

The good turns out to be what most people think desirable. So you get ethics by consensus, euthanasia if enough people vote for it, abortion if that's what people want. Actually this democracy of ethics is the death-knell of all we used to know as morality. Yet I see no way out of this on atheistic or agnostic presuppositions. Whence are you to derive a moral imperative?

The more you think about it, the more terrifying it becomes. I have no doubt that Russian leaders who incarcerate 'deviant' artists and thinkers in mental hospitals think they are doing it for the good of the community . . . and even for the good of the victims. And when the boot is on the other foot in right-wing Chile, doubtless they too think they are repressing dangerous elements in the community for love's sake and for the common good. It brings us back to Plato's question, 'Who will control the guardians?' If there is no absolute in morality, if there is no imperative outside ourselves which we have an unconditional duty to obey, we are indeed in a morass of relativism, and love ceases to mean anything very much.

But once 'give me a point where I may stand and I will move the world', as Archimedes put it, and a very different picture emerges. Love is an absolute for us Christians.

69

Indeed, it is *the* absolute, because it is the projection into our world of what God is. God is love, and he showed it not by making genial noises about us, nor by showering us with benefits. He showed how much he loved us by what he was willing to endure for us. He measured love by sacrifice. 'God so loved the world that he gave his only Son . . .' for us. So that is what love means: total self-giving for the good of the other. A self-giving that does not count the cost. A self-giving that does not even demand response. It comes to us with no strings attached. There are plenty who spit in the eye of such love. But those who allow themselves to be warmed by it turn into new creatures, children of the Love-king. They may often fall from that high ideal. They certainly will, being human and fallible. But they have within their grasp the principle of their reform. The Scriptures, which bear testimony to the love which became incarnate, will refashion them and make them more like their source.

I believe that history shows us that morality does not long survive the decease of religion in any society. Trotsky discovered this too late, when he was battered to death by those who pursued the amoral utilitarian principles he had himself taught. It happened in both Greece and Rome. Moral decline set in, despite all the official advocacy of the highest ideals, when the fires of religion died. It happened with ancient Israel: they abandoned God, and their morals decayed very soon, and we find them surrendering to the licence and cruelty of nature worship. In England the collapse of morals has consistently gone hand in hand with rejection of God. It was so at the Restoration. It was so in the eighteenth century. It certainly is so today, as crime soars and riots begin in the street about a generation after the widespread collapse of faith in the country. Many thoughtful Germans recognize it to be true of their fatherland: they see the link between the rejection of God in the thirties and the horrors of the concentration camps in the forties. The theologian Emil Brunner summarized the point well:

The feeling for the personal and the human which is the fruit of faith may outlive for a time the death of the roots from which it has grown. But this cannot last very long. As a rule the decay of religion works out in the second generation as moral rigidity and in the third generation as the breakdown of all morality. Humanity without religion has never been a historical force capable of resistance. Dehumanisation results.

Is that not true? Does it not emphasize that love without God, morals without religion, are impossible in the long run?

How is love possible?

But even if motivation was high and love was fully understood, I should still have a problem. I should want to ask my humanist friend how he proposes to achieve this desirable outcome of a loving world. Where is the power to come from?

I suppose one answer, frequently given, would be education. But is that not wildly optimistic? I have been in education all my life, but I could not honestly say that I have seen standards either of learning or of ethics rising during that period. And is it true, anyway, that if you educate someone you necessarily make him a better person? Could education not turn him into a more dangerous crook? What are we to make of the fact that the last two global wars have taken place among the most highly educated countries of the world? What are we to make of the fact that the decent majority in one of those countries capitulated to Hitler's destructive magnetism and perpetrated some of the most horrendous and extensive atrocities in history? Education seems to have slipped up a bit there.

The illusion that education will make us all good and loving is a very old one and very disastrous. It goes back at least as far as Plato. He thought and taught at one stage in his life that nobody willingly goes wrong. But that was before he was hired as the tutor for a little ruffian destined to be the tyrant of Syracuse! The great man retired, crestfallen. He had discovered that education does not produce virtue.

But if education will not eradicate the evil in human

71

nature, what will? Perhaps you don't think there is any evil in human nature? Just misfortune, poor background and being misunderstood? Well, what do you make of someone like the Yorkshire Ripper? Perfectly sane, but utterly wicked: he set out consistently to rape and kill, and he was highly successful at it. And do you suppose prison will change that sort of character for the better? Alas, that is practically never the case. People generally come out of our prisons worse than when they went into them. There needs to be something more powerful than constraint to induce moral, loving behaviour.

Perhaps effort will do it? Disciplined living and trying hard? I fear not. That again is an escape route from the challenge of Christ. History is eloquent with the testimony of people who have tried to live a good life and found that it was beyond them. Herodotus, 'the father of history', admitted, 'One of the greatest woes among mortal men is this, that although we attempt so much that is good, we do not achieve it.' The Roman love poet Ovid expressed the same point pungently in his famous epigram: 'I see the better course, and I approve it, but I follow the worse.' That is just the trouble. Though, come to think of it, it is worse than that: all too often we do not even seek the better course.

Some years ago I was in touch with an able and militantly anti-Christian humanist. She wrote to me after one of our discussions: 'Why do I need God to help me control my faults? Shouldn't I rather strive to better myself? I've tried that for a year now, and succeeded mostly, except during exams . . . I have tried to excuse this as abnormal but I can't. So I'll try harder.' Tremendously high standards, yes. Lots of effort. But it did not work. Six months later she wrote, 'I feel so selfish always working and slaving away for myself, and even though I swore I could in the old days force myself to become a much nicer person, all through willpower, I find I can't. I'm too lazy, and I never get round to it.'

That is precisely the problem. The power is lacking. Paul knew that. 'I do not do the good I want, but the evil I do not want is what I do' (Romans 7:19). Wrong comes so much more naturally to us than right. We need some power to counteract it effectively, because left to ourselves we would either never get round to the good we intend or, if we did, we would become impossibly self-opinionated.

The Jesus alternative

But this is just where Christianity is so relevant. Jesus Christ taught the very highest ideals – *and kept them*. And his offer and promise to his followers was this. He would come by his Spirit into the lives of any man, woman or child on this earth and take up residence there. He would then begin to start living out his life in them and through them. It would not come out pure and unmixed, because his sparkling nectar is dispensed from such a filthy cup. Our behaviour as Christians is such a mix of his love working through us and our own selfishness getting in the way. Nevertheless the spring of love is there, and it does not ever run dry. The God of love who made us, died for us, now lives in us, and provides not simply the motive and demonstration but the power to go on loving. The Christian humanist has nothing to boast about, least of all over his non-Christian colleague who may be a better person and may try a good deal harder. The main difference is this. The Christian has looked into the eyes of unconditional love. 'God's own love is shed abroad in his heart through the Holy Spirit given to him' (Romans 5:5), and he can't keep quiet about the discovery. He has found the cure to the perennial wickedness of the human heart. It lies in first being bathed and then energized by the love which flows from Calvary. It makes a difference. And we are not kidding ourselves. Such love can stand up to the hardest circumstances. Hear Mother Teresa of Calcutta:

> I have found the paradox that if I love until it hurts, then there is no hurt, but only more love. As I held and fed the morsel of life that was an aborted baby, as I held the hand of a man dying of cancer and felt his trust and gratitude, I could see, feel and touch God's love which has existed from the beginning.

11
Does science discredit Christianity?

The man in the street reckons that science has killed religion.
A good deal of what he sees on the television screen
confirms him in that assumption. And when he walks to his
favourite pub round the corner and passes the local church,
its general state of repair, its notice-board, and the people
who go there do nothing to change his views. Between
science and religion there is a great gulf; the one is modern
and the other old-fashioned; the one works and the other
does not.

This attitude is not altogether surprising; we live in an age
of phenomenal change. The horse and buggy has given way
to the space shuttle in less than a century. But is the objection well founded? Is there a basic incompatibility between
Christianity and science?

1. THE HARMONY BETWEEN CHRISTIANITY
AND SCIENCE

The debt of science to Christianity

We need to recall at the outset that the growth of modern
science took place in the cradle of a Christian civilization,
recently liberated from authoritarianism by the Renaissance
and given new motivation by the Reformation. It could
hardly have originated anywhere else.

If you are going to pursue the natural sciences, you need
certain conditions. First, a conviction that the material world

74

exists and is important: and you would scarcely have found that in the East where material things are thought to be either illusory or unimportant. Then again, you need the freedom to examine the evidence, wherever it may lead you. And that freedom was to be found primarily in countries where dogma had been submitted to the Word of God. Third, all scientific advance depends upon certain assumptions, such as the uniformity of nature and the principle of cause and effect. Without these axioms science cannot proceed. It was therefore no accident that the natural sciences, as we know them, were born in Christian Europe.

The early scientists were Christians to a man. Galileo and Copernicus remained devout believers, convinced that their work glorified God, despite the provocation afforded them by the Catholic Church of the day. Newton wrote his *Principia* in the assurance that 'this world could originate from nothing but the perfectly free will of God', and is said to have spent as much time in Bible study as in scientific research. Kepler, who revolutionized the astronomical prejudice, derived from Plato, that there are only circular movements among the planets, felt that he was 'thinking God's thoughts after him'. He was 'a high priest in the book of nature, religiously bound to alter not one jot or tittle of what it had pleased God to write down in it'. That is why he took very seriously the 8 minutes of divergence from the circular in Mars' orbit, which he discovered *by observation,* and thereby paved the way for the reformation of astronomy. Francis Bacon, one of the earliest scientists, saw God as the author of two books: his words in Scripture and his works in nature. Both were facets of his self-disclosure.

This idea of the two books, the book of nature and the book of Scripture, has a lot to be said for it. Indeed, the parallels between the two are most striking. Here are a few of them.

1. *Both teach the contingency of the universe.* It might be other than it is. Why is it what it is? The scientist believes that the truths about nature must be found out through observation; they are not necessary truths which can be dis-

covered by reason alone. The speed of light, for instance, might be something different. Science can give no reason for the world being as it is. It is dependent, contingent. But contingent on what? Science is not competent to answer such questions. Instead it points beyond itself. Scripture also teaches that the universe is contingent; but it tells us on what – the unfettered will of the Creator (Revelation 4:11; Isaiah 40:13f.).

2. *Both imply that the universe had a beginning and will have an end.* We live between the Big Bang and the death of the solar system. At least, that is what the present data appear to suggest. There is little anticipation in scientific circles that the universe will be eternal. That chimes in very much with the biblical teaching that neither man nor his universe is eternal by nature; both have a beginning and an end. Unpleasant though it may be, it is unwise to run away from reflection about the end.

3. *Both assume that reality is governed by law.* Scientists are continually, and very successfully, seeking to explain the multifarious variety of phenomena in terms of fixed and universal laws. When these laws are flouted, chaos results. On the other hand, this is precisely what we refuse to accept in the moral realm. Everyone demands the right to do his own thing. But the Scriptures insist that there are principles of right conduct, and predict chaos if these are broken: 'Do not be deceived; God is not mocked, for whatever a man sows, that he will also reap' (Galatians 6:7).

4. *Both teach the importance of authority.* It must not be thought that science is anti-authoritarian and free-thinking. Nothing could be further from the truth. What released science at the Renaissance was not the repudiation of authority as such, but the exchange of a fallible and arbitrary authority (the great names of antiquity like Aristotle and Galen) for the God-given authority of his revelation in nature, appealed to by careful experiment. Science stands or falls by this common allegiance to one final court of appeal. It may take time and much experiment to come to a common mind, but there is no doubt where final authority lies. It lies in what *is*; what can be measured, observed, weighed,

compared. It lies in the God given authority of his revelation in Scripture — an authority, incidentally, which Jesus Christ recognized and to which he appealed. God's word is true, and under scrutiny we find that it matches our experience of reality. It may take time and much discussion to see the current application of Scripture on any particular point, but its authority is not in doubt. Both science and Christianity teach that there is a final authority: it is important to find it and abide by it.

5. *Both insist on the objectivity of truth*. The scientist does not dream up his data. He does not spin them out of his own mind. They are not necessarily what he would wish. But they are sacred and inviolate. All scientists believe in the importance of 'givenness'. Loyalty to the data afforded by the natural world enables the scientist to stand on common ground with colleagues everywhere. Without such loyalty, reality would disintegrate into subjectivity and imagination. It is much the same with Christianity. It presents us with data, with a certain givenness: not what we have dreamed up, not necessarily what we like, but given to us. The God who wrote the objectivity of truth so clearly into the natural world tells us in Scripture that we tend to hide from the truth, and so he has himself come to disclose the truth to us: 'I am the truth' (John 14:6).

6. *Both spotlight the fallenness of human nature*. Science does so by inference, Scripture by assertion. Why do we quail at the possibilities of germ warfare or a nuclear holocaust? The power which split the atom could well be harnessed to beneficial use for mankind. Why does genetic engineering seem so terrifying? It could well manipulate bacteria into producing useful substances. There is nothing sinister in the advance of knowledge as such. The sinister thing is human nature which can so easily misuse it. The perversity of human nature, not the inventiveness of the scientist, is the basic trouble. But we run away from that conclusion, too. It draws us irresistibly in the direction of the biblical teaching that 'the heart is deceitful above all things, and desperately sick' (Jeremiah 17:9).

7. *Both assert the importance of integrity.* You must genuinely seek. And when you find, you must commit yourself to the results and check your conclusions by further experiment. It will not do to cook the results. Sooner or later the culprit's lack of integrity is revealed, and the outcome can be disastrous. This is precisely the emphasis of Scripture. We are told we must seek the Lord with our whole heart: he is there to be found. The evidence lies plain before us in Jesus of Nazareth. We are then called to go where the evidence points, and commit ourselves to the hypothesis that he is willing and able to enter our lives: we must then confirm that hypothesis by the further experiment of living with him. Anything less is cooking the results. Integrity is essential.

8. *Both require community and discipline.* Reality is too vast for any one person to comprehend it adequately. Co-operation is a notable and necessary characteristic of the scientific community. The examination and collation of facts, their interpretation and checking, need the stimulus and interplay of other minds. There is a subtle blend of individual responsibility and the discipline of submission to the judgment of colleagues; both are needed. And the success of the scientific community in this area is an example to the rest of society with its increasing fragmentation and individualism. Science mirrors the interplay of individual responsibility and corporate belonging which marks the New Testament teaching about the Christian church.

Here, then, are eight ways in which there is a discernible harmony between the approach of the natural sciences and of the Christian faith. Frankly, if we do not like them, it could be because the book of nature and the book of Scripture point in the same direction – from which we are on the run. Who wants to be reminded of law and authority, the objectivity of truth and the fallenness of man? But at least it should be plain that there exists no necessary hostility between Christianity and science.

Ways of knowing

If there is a great similarity in scientific and Christian

approaches, there is also an important difference. Basically, there are three kinds of knowledge, mathematical, scientific and personal. Each type is similar in that it proceeds from presuppositions which are eminently sensible but cannot be proved. Mathematical knowledge requires the assumption of axioms and of meaningfulness. Scientific knowledge requires the assumption that there is an external world and that there is uniformity in nature's behaviour. Personal knowledge requires the assumption that there are other people to be met. We are so accustomed to making the acts of faith which these assumptions demand, that we do not even notice we are doing it.

Now whereas mathematical knowledge has no necessary relationship with the outside world, the other two have. But they operate differently. You do not put your girl-friend into a test-tube to determine her chemical constituents. You take her out for the evening instead! Scientific knowledge analyses and describes. Personal knowledge meets and relates. The two are different, but complementary. They are not in competition with each other. And religious knowledge belongs to the personal variety. So whereas scientific knowledge is concerned with description, religious knowledge is concerned with encounter. Science is concerned with the material aspect of things, but religion belongs to the world of personal relationships. Like all personal knowledge it is not merely encounter: a relationship ensues once we get to know someone. It is like that with God.

So science and religion are not mutually hostile claimants to be the only proper path to knowledge. They are perfectly compatible and complementary. The proper sphere of science is to look into the 'how' and the 'what' of God's creation: the sphere of religious enquiry is to ask 'how come?' and 'what for?'. Truth is unitive, and so the Christian may embrace science to find out how God has worked in this world, and the scientist may embrace faith in order to find the purpose and encounter the origin of all there is, in God himself.

2. THE HOSTILITY BETWEEN CHRISTIANITY AND SCIENCE

But granted it is perfectly logical to be a good Christian and a good scientist, the question remains, why has there been such hostility between the two approaches? Why have relationships over the past century been bedevilled by so much mis-understanding and arrogance?

Pride and prejudice

In its pronouncements about science the church has often adopted a dogmatic stance which has boomeranged savagely. Its opposition to Copernicus' heliocentric theory of the universe is a classic example. But the Christian believes — or should believe — that the God of grace is also the God of nature, and that truth from whatsoever source is welcome.

The Bible is not a scientific book. It never sets out to be. It is a book which speaks of man's relation to himself, to the world, and to God. Insofar as it enters into the scientific field at all, it does so in ordinary everyday language which speaks of the sun as 'rising' (when it does nothing of the sort) or the heavens as being 'up' (when that is manifestly too restrictive). We do in fact talk like that: so does the Bible. It does not attempt to speak in scientific terms. If it had; it would have remained incomprehensible to the majority of mankind until our own day. So it is sheer arrogance, and misplaced arro-gance at that, for the Christian believer to tell the scientist what he may or may not believe about the physical universe, on the grounds of a particular interpretation of the Bible. On the contrary, the Bible encourages us to believe that God wants us to seek out the secrets of his universe and govern it with justice and humility under him.

So there is no excuse for the Christian to run away from science. He will welcome truth wherever it is found. He will expect scientific discovery to cohere with the teaching of Scripture, because he is convinced that one God of truth is the author of both. When he meets discrepancies, he will do two things: First, as a scientist, he will re-examine the infer-

80

ences he has drawn from his discovery. Then, as a Christian, he will re-examine his own interpretation of Scripture. And often he will have to admit he does not know.

The church has had no monopoly of arrogance and misunderstanding. The very success of the scientific method has so elated some of its practitioners that they have given the impression that theirs was the only approach to reality, and that anything which would not fit into a test-tube or could not be measured was not real!

Bertrand Russell's *Why I am not a Christian* shows something of this arrogance. On the one hand, since belief in God, immortality and the like are unsupported by science, they must, he maintains, be discarded. On the other, 'Science can enable our grandchildren to live a good life, by giving them knowledge, self-control, and characters productive of harmony rather than strife.' Now is not that as arrant nonsense as any bishop ever pronounced against science? Russell's grandchildren will be lucky if they survive this century at all, bristling as it is with arsenals of nuclear weaponry, let alone enjoy the good life of self-discipline and harmony given them by science. Try 'self-discipline and harmony' for size on the present social and international scene!

No, it ill befits Christians like Archbishop Ussher to inform the scientists that the world was made in 4004 BC; or scientists, even with the support of intellectuals of the stature of Lord Russell, to adopt the mantle of Prometheus. Pride and prejudice are real obstacles both for scientific and for religious advance. They have no place in either.

The God of the gaps

A second reason for the poor relations between Christianity and science is the tendency there has been in Christian circles to claim room for God only in areas where human knowledge has not yet reached. This 'God of the gaps' is a pathetic travesty of the dynamic, infinite, all-pervasive God revealed to us in the Bible. There he is portrayed as both immanent within the universe ('in him we live and move and have our being', Acts 17:28) and also immeasurably greater ('dwelling in unapproachable light. No man has ever seen or ever can see him', 1 Timothy 6:16). To shrink God until he is invoked only to cover the ever-decreasing gaps in our knowledge is blasphemous. Such a God is too small to be worthy of anyone's worship.

Either God is there in every detail of the universe or he is not there at all. It was the rationalists who made the mistake of supposing that God's existence hung on whether he could be discerned in some part or other of the world, a fallacy perpetuated by the first Russian cosmonaut who came back claiming that God was clearly unreal because he had not met him during his trip through space! It is a similar sort of error to supposing that an artist is unreal unless you can see him somewhere or other in his own canvas. The truth is that the canvas, though internally self-explanatory, would not be there at all were it not for the artist who has in fact manifested himself in every brush-stroke.

The God whom Christians believe in holds the world in his hands. He upholds the whole universe 'by his word of power' (Hebrews 1:3). In him we live and move and have our being, 'since he himself gives to all men life and breath and everything' (Acts 17:25). 'Every single thing was created through, and for, him. He is both the first principle and the upholding principle of the whole scheme of creation' (Colossians 1:16–17, Phillips). He is the God of the physical universe every bit as much as he is Lord of human hearts. He is the God who makes possible both scientific discovery and religious faith.

The disastrous debate

If pride and prejudice, coupled with a concept of 'God of the gaps', have been two of the problems in the relation of science to Christianity, undoubtedly the third and most influential has been the issue of evolution. The Bible is seen to teach creation in six days; Darwin proposed continuous evolution. That is how it appears to the average non-scientist. And since 1860 it has been so much the worse for the Bible.

On the Origin of Species had come out in 1859, but it was in the next year that the fur flew. The British Association met in Oxford to discuss the theory. Bishop Samuel Wilberforce of Oxford violently opposed it because he thought it inconsistent with Scripture, and ended his address by asking Professor T. H. Huxley whether it was through his grandfather or his grandmother that he claimed descent from a monkey. Huxley replied by expounding Darwin's arguments and concluded that he would not be ashamed to have a monkey as an ancestor, but that he would be ashamed to be connected with someone who used great gifts to obscure the truth! The debate was indeed disastrous and has had disastrous consequences. For the ordinary person it has meant that there appears to be an unbridgeable divide between Christianity and science. For the sciences it has meant a large degree of isolation from the insights and values which the Christian faith, and indeed the early chapters of Genesis, can offer. For the church it has meant widespread confusion, many secessions, and splits among Christians ranging from an insular fundamentalism that sticks to the literal interpretation of Genesis 1–3 to a liberalism, such as that put forward by Teilhard de Chardin, which sees God as thoroughly involved in the evolutionary process but which has little use for the Bible. There have been no winners in this deplorable and quite unnecessary battle.

I say 'unnecessary' advisedly. For there is a variety of literary form in the Scriptures – poetry, history, proverb, fable, epistle and the like. Some Christians suppose that the Genesis account of creation is straight reportage, the sort of thing a journalist might have written down had he been there. Others feel that, quite apart from a snake that talks and weeds that grow only after the Fall, there is no earthly reason why it *should* be literal history. In any case, the literary genre is not crucial. The pictorial language of Genesis 1–3 is one thing; the teaching it embodies is another. And the teaching is powerful and unequivocal. It maintains that the whole universe derives from God the Creator; that man is at the same time part of the animal world ('formed of dust from the ground') and also shares God's 'breath of life' and bears his 'image'. There is, in other words, a continuity and a discontinuity between man and the animal world.

Furthermore, the teaching of these chapters is that man was intended to harness and use natural resources (1:28), to work, with a weekly day off (2:15; 2:3) and to exercise a responsible stewardship over the creation (2:15). The chapters go further, and show that man used his free will to reject God; that this was the cause of all his disarray, that God loves man still and has made a way for his 'nakedness to be covered', but that the world can no longer remain a 'garden'. It is hard to imagine a more effective tool than the graphic Genesis story for bringing home these profound truths to a world full of diverse understandings and cultures.

Now there is nothing here to which a scientist, as scientist, should object. There need be no conflict between evolution and the doctrine of Genesis 1 and 2. And it is the *doctrine* of the Bible that Christians want to discover and live by, irrespective of the literary clothes in which it is dressed.

Creation and evolution

But are not creation and evolution mutually exclusive? Well, some scientists and some Christians think so. There has been a great revival of anti-evolutionary creationism in the United States recently, and tempers run high on both sides. It is perhaps fair to say that much of the evidence is ambiguous and depends either on circular argument (you date the fossils by the rocks they are in, and the rocks by the fossils they contain!) or by extrapolation (from minor genetic changes to major developments in species). A number of respectable scientists support creationism on the basis of the scientific evidence. But undeniably the majority of scientists believe in some form of evolutionary process, though they differ considerably on how it came about. A good deal of rethinking is going on at present, as scientists discover that some quite fundamental assumptions (of chemical evolution especially) were wrong. So the popular presentation of Darwinian evolutionary theory as unquestionable truth is oversimplified and is far from certain.

In what follows, however, I want to take the evolutionary

case very seriously. Most people accept it and most people think that it disproves the Bible. Let us then assume the basic truth of evolution and see whether it really does destroy the teaching of the Bible.

A couple of preliminary points are worth making. In the first place, if evolution is seen as 'development with difference', that need not put God out of business. Darwin himself said that it was a matter of indifference whether God breathed life into many forms or one.

Moreover, it is a serious logical mistake to contrast creation with evolution, though this is commonly done. Both are attempting to account for the origin and development of species. Evolution describes the process by which life develops; creation points to the prior act on which that process depends.

Chance — or creation?

But does not Darwinian theory assume random mutation in the forms of life? Does it not say, in effect, that chance is king? And if so, is that not totally at odds with the biblical picture which sees God's design in nature?

Let us look a bit more closely at this word, chance. Actually, 'chance' is an expression of our ignorance. Much that once seemed chance we now see to have a rational explanation. So we would be unwise to overplay it. Look down your microscope at the atoms in an orchid: they will appear random. But lift your eye from the microscope, take in the beauty and perfume of that orchid, and design will be no less apparent! Physical laws do hold good in our world, even though their basis may be 'chance' at the microscopic level. What appears to be 'chance' in the light of our limited observation may be part of a grand design which we are just too small to cope with.

All this need cause the Christian no embarrassment. Rather the reverse. It is thrilling to imagine that the element of randomness in the universe allows (given enough space and time) every possible state of life to be explored. That is creation indeed! It is breath taking in its awesomeness and majesty. How small God would be if he could work only through principles which we fully understood. As a matter of fact, chance is often shown in Scripture to be one of the tools God uses. A classic exámple is the death of Ahab, king of Israel. He had been given a prophecy that he was to die in the forthcoming battle at Ramoth-gilead. So he went into the battle in disguise. But that did not help him. 'A certain man drew his bow at a venture, and struck the king of Israel between the scale armour and the breastplate' (1 Kings 22:34). And that was the end of him. God's plan was achieved by the most random of human chances!

So why should we not see God both as Creator, and also as working, at least partly, through mutation and selection? Why should we not describe this book you are reading as both a product of my design and also a pattern of chemically-known molecules?

We can take this analogy further. Why should the author not be allowed to adjust his plot if he so wishes? Christians believe God has done just that: in the original creation of something out of nothing, in the creation of animal life, and in the creation of man in his own image. It is perfectly possible to combine this conviction with acceptance of evolution. To be sure, it is hard for us to reconcile the messy, bloody and wasteful process of evolution with the goodness of a creator God. But then it is hard for us to reconcile the fall of man, and the consequent mess we have made, with the purposes of God. Perhaps there's a link between the two? And could it be that our idea of God's love is too sugary? Does all this waste underline how high is the cost of freedom? Have we failed to see how at all levels life is rooted in sacrifice? Jesus himself, remember, is described as 'the Lamb slain from the foundation of the world' (Revelation 13:8, AV). And even if we are unable fully to reconcile the love of God as we understand it with evolution as we understand it, that need not rule out either of them. God's thoughts are by definition higher than ours; his ways are past finding out. If the evidence for evolution is good enough (and, while not compelling, it is very strong) we should accept that, provisionally. If the evidence for God's love is good enough (and it is utterly solid; the cross of Christ) then we should accept that, decisively. And if we are unable to make a fully satisfactory synthesis of the two, that may well be a mark of our finitude. We may just have to put up with it!

Six days – or millions of years?

The debate rages not merely over the emergence of life on earth, but on the time-scale. The biblical account indicates six days: the evolutionary requirement is millions of years. What are we to make of so glaring a contradiction? Well, the arguments derived from radioactive dating, the fossil record, the saltiness of the sea and magnetic orientation do indicate a very old earth. Individually these methods of calculation may be open to question, but collectively they are very strong indeed. The earth has clearly been around for a very long time.

But this need not be a problem to the Christian. The word 'day' has a variety of meanings in the Bible. 'Twenty-four hours' is the usual meaning, but often it means an era or epoch, and this is probably how we should understand the Genesis reference, particularly since sun and moon, day and night, do not appear until the fourth day! And when we are talking about time we should never forget our human limitations, and the God who transcends them. 'With the Lord one day is as a thousand years, and a thousand years as one day' (2 Peter 3:8; cf. Psalm 90:4).

Naked ape – or divine image?

A third contentious area concerns man himself. What are we to think of him? Genesis says 'the LORD God formed man of dust from the ground, and breathed into his nostrils the breath of life; and man became a living being' (2:7). That is to say, man is unambiguously part of the physical world. Genesis shows him as the crown of a sequence which accords exactly with evolutionary theory: matter, water, plants, animals, and finally man. But there is more to man than that! God 'breathed into his nostrils the breath of life': mental and

87

spiritual life, as well as physical. Moreover, 'God created man in his own image' (Genesis 1:27). That 'image' includes all the ways in which we transcend the animals: notably an awareness of God, a conscience alert to right and wrong, an appreciation of beauty and truth, and the ability to think and to pray. Somewhere along the evolutionary process God put this 'image', this 'breath of life' into hominids, and they became men. That does not mean they were any different physiologically or physically: as a species man remained related to the apes. But he was qualitatively different. 'God has made everything beautiful in its time; he has also set eternity in the hearts of men' (Ecclesiastes 3:11).

But the story does not end there. The image of God has become tainted in us human beings, though it has not been totally erased. We have fallen back from union and friendship with God to below the level of the animal world. To call anyone a 'beast' or his behaviour 'bestial' is an insult to the animals! Nevertheless there remains in us an impression of that lost image, and a longing for it. This image can be restored through Jesus, who is 'the image of the God we cannot see' (Colossians 1:15).

What?, you say. How can you believe in the Fall of man when evolution is always moving in the opposite direction, from chaos into order? I do not find that objection insuperable. It is perfectly possible that man has evolved physically and mentally without there being any necessary development in his spiritual awareness and stature. There is remarkably little evidence for the moral progress of man: our own century, for all its education and sophistication, has seen greater greed, brutality, torture, starvation and mass murder than any other in all history. As T. H. Huxley put it in a more civilized era, 'The doctrines of the innate depravity of man appear to me to be vastly nearer the truth than the "liberal" popular illusions that all babies are born good, and that the example of a corrupt society is responsible for their failing to remain so.'

We have been looking, sketchily enough in all conscience, at some areas of a vast subject. It is so vast that it is improbable that universal agreement will ever be reached. Much

88

must remain unknown, much hypothetical. But there is no reason to suppose that science, and the Christian faith which gave it birth, are irreconcilable. That is simply not the case. All too often fancied disagreements between Christianity and science are used as excuses to evade the challenge of Jesus Christ. And that is a great pity. For the true scientist has the deepest respect for truth. He does not run away from uncomfortable possibilities. So he will examine the Gospels for himself. He will concentrate on the questions 'Who is this Jesus?' and 'Did he rise from the dead?' And when he is clear where the evidence points, he will have the courage to commit himself, and to follow wherever it leads.

12
Does Christianity make any difference?

'Well, suppose I did become a Christian. What difference would it make?' Haven't you heard questions like that? There is a deeply held assumption in many circles that Christianity has nothing of any importance to say to our modern world, that it is supported by only the very old or the very naïve, and that for all practical purposes it is as dead as a dodo.

There is reason for such cynicism. Christianity has been around for nearly two thousand years and the world is in a bigger mess than it has ever been. The church at large seems to be rather like the United Nations – good men and true seeking to make the world a better place but passing rather ineffectual resolutions which don't actually achieve anything. As for the church round the corner, well, we know Mrs Jones who goes there. It does not seem to make a great difference to her. Very much the same programme seems to take place every week. The service goes on whether people turn up or not, whether they believe or not.

No, Christianity seems to make little difference at either the corporate or the individual level. We can well do without it.

Our society

But wait a moment. We, who can do without Christianity, are not in very good shape, are we? In most of the developing countries of the world there is scandalously unjust distribution of wealth, oppressive government, illiteracy, poor medical care, widespread poverty, corruption and famine. In most of the first-world countries there is a cluster of problems — inflation, unemployment, loneliness, fear, breakdown of relationship, and a corrosive and unsatisfying materialism. My own country, Britain, has lost an empire and failed to discover a role in the world. Production is low. Strikes are high. We are consumed by our domestic concerns of unemployment and inflation. Yet we are always clamouring for more money, and we are quite prepared to tread on others in order to get it. We are profoundly self-indulgent. We spend as much on gambling as on the defence budget. Nearly half the hospital beds in our creaking National Health Service are occupied by patients with psychological rather than physical ailments. Illegitimacy, abortion and AIDS soar. Divorce affects someone in almost every family, and it is the children who suffer most. Eighty percent of all crime comes from broken homes, and we have the highest crime rate in our history. Prisons groan with three men to a single cell. The queues for the courts get longer and longer. All the traditional virtues are at a discount and apathy and smugness reign, O.K. We don't need Christianity. It is irrelevant!

Our panaceas: education . . .

Instead we have our patent cures. Education is one panacea. If only we are better educated we will be able to put the world to rights. Really? We've already met this idea (on page 71) and noticed that the best-educated societies in the world constitute the biggest threat to the continued life of mankind on this planet. How is it that, when we know perfectly well (because we have been educated) that the average Peruvian earns about £100 per annum, we do nothing about it and care less — except when the price of coffee goes up? In point of fact, the pursuit of education is far more pragmatic. It is in order to get a better job (or to get a job at all), so as to earn more money for the education of our own young . . . If you think about that, it implies that there is no ultimate meaning for mankind — or for education.

... technology

Technology is another blind alley. We have a pathetic confidence in the experts to come up with a technical answer to the problems of our society. But most of the biggest problems are not susceptible of technical answers. Technology will do nothing to alter apartheid in South Africa, suppression of the intelligentsia in Russia or self-indulgence in the West. Scientific discovery on its own will not lead us to paradise. Rather, the reverse. It has placed in our hands the most terrifying weapons of destruction, so much so that one nuclear missile contains more explosive power than all the TNT used in the Second World War, and mankind has the ability to blast the world to smithereens ten times over. We are good at terminating pregnancies, and murder millions in that way, because we find it convenient. We will soon be expert at eliminating the elderly – painlessly and humanely. It is not the technology we need to be worried about; it is human nature. Mankind is not to be trusted with ultimate power over others. The state is not to be trusted. And we would be totally misguided to put our faith in the technocrats. When the first nuclear bomb was exploded in 1945 Enrico Ferni, one of the inventors, said, 'Forget your scruples; the thing's superb physics.' To place our faith in technology could be the ultimate folly. Steve Turner put it superbly in his poem, 'In the End'.

> In the end
> in the very end of the last moment
> when the filter tip of the world
> is completely shadowed by a descending
> hell, we'll call in the experts
> for their considered opinion.
> We'll arrange for an apocalyptic
> edition of *Time Magazine*,
> complete with artists' impressions.
> We'll comfort ourselves with the fact
> that it has never happened before.
> In the end we'll be deciding

whether to decide.
In the very end of the last moment
we'll falter, half believing,
half crushed.

... psychiatry

In the light of this haunting fear of cosmic destruction which underlies every other malaise of our day, vast numbers of people turn to psychiatrists. The psychiatrist enjoys the respect which the parson and the politician used to have; though, curiously, people are still ashamed of going to consult him. The psychiatrist with his drugs or analysis can be a real help in calming a patient and disentangling tangles in his life. What he cannot do is to impart a new power. 'Even after complete and successful analysis the patient still has no more than his own resources to rely on', wrote Stafford Clark, himself a practising psychiatrist. 'Thrown back on himself he finds no comfort in self-sufficiency. This is the crisis in analysis, and within its own framework analysis has no answer. The patient cannot get it from the analyst, and if he could it would not last a lifetime. Where does he turn? As a psychiatrist I do not know. As a man I can only say "I believe in God".'

Education, technology, psychiatry: none of these is an adequate resource for twentieth-century people baffled and submerged by problems in ourselves and our environment which are surely greater than in any previous generation. If these trusted remedies are not effective, what hope is there that the old medicine distilled at Bethlehem and Calvary will do any good?

What can Jesus do?

Let us be clear what we are talking about. I am not saying that formal churchianity has anything very profound to contribute to the healing of the modern world. I am not claiming that religion which assumes it is Christian because it is nothing else has anything to offer. Not the Christianity of 'try

93

hard and lead as good a life as you can', nor the Christianity of an intellectual system or a set of values. True Christianity is Christ. He came to this world in order to help us – to rescue us, no less. He died in order to distil the medicine for our most malignant disease, self-centredness. He rose again to share his life with us. It is possible to know him. It is possible to be changed by him. I have seen it happen to people of every background in every continent.

Very well, what difference can he make?

Breakdown of relationship

Think of the breakdown of relationship: between husband and wife, parent and child, union and management. Jesus Christ is alive: he does change lives. And therefore he changes relationships. Time and again I have seen marriages repaired once the warring partners have allowed Jesus Christ access to their lives. Time and again I have seen the same thing happen between parents and children.

It happens in industry too. One of the remarkable men I met in Pittsburgh, U.S.A., the centre of the steel industry, was Wayne Alderson. The effect this man had on a steel mill that was in the midst of a bitter strike and was losing money hand over fist, was remarkable. He was a Christian, and he approached the problems with Christ. He helped to faith one of the leading Union officials, and together the two of them pulled the factory round. They taught the Sermon on the Mount in the lunch-breaks. Their relationships with one another and with the work-force utterly transformed an ugly situation. Within a year the mill was working harmoniously, and many of the workers had come to Christ (so had their wives, amazed at the difference Christ had made to their husbands). And Alderson was sacked – for bringing Christianity into industry!

It is impossible to exaggerate this reconciling power of Christ, so sorely needed in our world today. Chuck Colson, who was mentioned earlier on (see page 18), recalls a night of Christian fellowship he spent, some time after his release from prison, with three other men with whom he would normally have had nothing to do – were it not for their common relationships to Christ. The first was Senator Harold Hughes, a reformed alcoholic and totally opposed to Colson politically. The second was Eldridge Cleaver, until recently the Marxist-Leninist leader of the Black Panthers, who had been dedicated to violent revolution and whom Colson had been trying to hunt down for years. He too had recently professed faith in Christ, disenchanted at last with other ideologies. The third was Tommy Tarrants, who was currently serving a long sentence as former leader of the Ku-Klux-Klan. He had specialized in blowing up the homes of blacks and Jews – until he too turned to Christ. It would have been hard to find four men more naturally opposed to all that each other stood for than these four men, but Colson tells how the love of Christ forged a wonderful bond between them. 'Nothing can divide men if we have the love of Christ in our hearts' was his summary of that experience. It is difficult to deny it.

Insecurity

Insecurity is another killer. It lies behind the shy and the brash alike. You find it in school leavers, in first-home buyers, in old folks. You find it in soldiers in combat, in shop assistants, in lovers. The uncertainty, the anxiety gnaws away at the stem of our lives, and the flower wilts accordingly. Very often our insecurity stems from early days, when we were offered love and acceptance by our parents and teachers, but only provided we behaved the way they wanted. What we need is love without strings attached. That is the warm climate in which we can develop in the way we should. But where do you find unconditional love? It is a very rare commodity.

I know only one place where it is always to be found: in the heart of God who came to this earth in order to draw the likes of you and me back to himself. 'I will never fail you nor forsake you,' he declares. 'Hence we can confidently say, "The Lord is my helper, I will not be afraid; what can man do to me?"' (Hebrews 13:5f.). The Lord's unconditional love is the thing that brings a deep security to the Christian. Jesus

95

did not simply say 'I love you'. He acted. He stretched wide his arms for us upon that cross, and cried, 'Father, forgive them, for they know not what they do' (Luke 23:34). That is how I can be sure of his love, however great my failings. That is how I can face the future unperturbed. There is no life-insurance attitude in authentic Christianity. There is no question of paying your premium on earth in order to gain a mansion in the skies. No. The Christian is totally insecure so far as the changes and chances of this mortal life are concerned; but he is doubly secure, none the less. He is secure because he knows that no circumstances can separate him from Jesus, 'the friend who sticks closer than a brother' (see Proverbs 18:24). And even if he gets killed, and that is the worst anyone can do to him, he does not lose out: his Lord has promised, 'Where I am you shall be also' (John 14:3). Listen to one man looking captivity and death steadily in the face:

> I am sure that neither death, nor life, nor angels, nor principalities, nor things present, nor things to come, nor powers, nor height, nor depth, nor anything else in all creation, will be able to separate us from the love of God in Christ Jesus our Lord. (Romans 8:38f.)

And millions of Christians have lived and died with that quiet assurance. Christ does make a profound difference to our insecurity as persons and to our uncertainties about the future.

Aimlessness

Aimlessness is one of the most notable features of modern life. You find it in the disintegration which happens when people are unemployed or retired. You find it equally in the hectic round of business with which the successful fill their lives. Sartre's words in *Nausea* are painfully near the mark. 'I was just thinking that here we are, all of us, eating and drinking to preserve our precious existence, and there's nothing, nothing, absolutely no reason for existing.' You find it in the playwrights: the most famous example of meaninglessness is Beckett's *Waiting for Godot*. He expresses this sardonically in *Endgame*. As an unspecified something takes place, Hamm asks 'We're not beginning to . . to . . mean something?' and Clov replies with a laugh, 'Mean something! You and I mean something!'

This widespread attitude is not altogether surprising. If this world had no creator and therefore has no purpose; if it sprang from nothing and will return to nothing in due course, the same must be true of every human being in it. Man without God cannot be expected to have much lasting purpose in life. Since all roads lead nowhere, it doesn't matter which of them you take. But everything changes dramatically if Jesus Christ goes down that road of life with you. If you get to know the God who is there, the God who has demonstrated himself in Jesus of Nazareth, why, then everything changes. The purpose of life is to know him and to enjoy him for ever. Our supreme aim will be to please him and to live for him. Our relationships, ambitions, time and energies will be geared towards knowing him and making him known. That is why many Christians seem intense and narrow-minded to their uncommitted friends. They have found treasure, and they want above all to share it. They may be crude and tactless about it, especially in their early attempts to tell others, but it is too good news to keep to themselves. Jesus Christ transforms the aimlessness of life. He gives a purpose which can be fulfilled in work and leisure, in employment and unemployment, in isolation and in community, in youth and in old age.

Discontent

Closely allied to aimlessness is discontent. Most people show symptoms of this unpleasantly contagious disease. It is most deeply rooted among those who have most possessions, and seems often to be almost absent in the poor of the earth. I have frequently contrasted the readiness to share and the readiness to laugh among African or Latin American poor with the greed and selfishness of European and North

97

American rich. Be that as it may, there is such a deep-rooted desire for more possessions in each one of us that the whole advertising industry gets rich by working on it. Their aim is to foster dissatisfaction. Generally it needs no fostering. The actress Raquel Welch expressed it with great honesty: 'I thought it was very peculiar that I had acquired everything I had wanted as a child; wealth, fame, success in my career. I had beautiful children and a lifestyle that seemed terrific. Yet I was totally and miserably unhappy.' Hollywood paints everything a bit larger than life, but it is easy for us to understand and share her feeling.

It is one of the paradoxes in life that the more we grab for money and possessions, success and fame, the more aware we are of the unsatisfied depths within. Even the more perceptive brewers realize this! One of them advertises its product as 'refreshing the parts other beers cannot reach'. Now, of course, no beer can have such potency as to assuage the depths of discontent in the human heart. But Christ can, and does. It comes almost as a shock to us when we find him offering his joy to his followers, so that their joy might be full (John 15:11). We have almost forgotten what joy is. We have mislaid it in our frenzied search for pleasures. And Christ wants to restore it to us, by bringing us into relationship with himself. Probably our highest conception of joy is relationship with another person to whom we are deeply attached. Christ will take that a stage further and give us the joy which comes from being in touch with God. Such joy lasts through loneliness and disappointment, through pain and bereavement. God gives it. Nobody can take it away. It makes a great deal of difference.

There are two other areas common to us all where Jesus Christ makes profound changes, and it is easy to experience this personally, even in the earliest days of Christian discipleship. The first is our sense of moral weakness, and the second our sense of guilt.

Moral bondage

One of the most obvious effects of coming to know Jesus

Christ is the way he releases us from various bondages to which we had been slaves. We are often not aware of them until we look into the perfect life of Jesus and see just how shop-soiled our life is. But other people are not blind to our besetting faults which grip us with invisible shackles. And even if, by dint of much concentration and effort, we succeed in getting rid of some of them, others rapidly replace them.

Now it is very evident that Christians remain far from perfect. But it is undeniable that Christ can and does break these invisible shackles of bad habits in the lives of those who entrust themselves to him. In his book *Is Anyone There?* David Watson gives an excellent example of the liberation Christ brings even in the most depressing circumstances. He tells of his visit to one of the top-security prisons, his meeting with John, who had recently become a Christian in his cell, and the letter he subsequently received from him. It bears repetition:

> This is my fifth time in prison. I am serving eight years for fraud. I was dirty outside my body and I never used to wash. I was dirty inside my heart; lust, hatred, greed, revenge, anger and malice.

He tells how he met with Jesus Christ, and the difference it made:

> I was able to stop reading dirty books. I was able to stop using dirty words, and the greatest of all, I was able to love the people whom I had hated. I felt a completely different person, like being born again, and this is the great work of our Lord Jesus Christ. I was really cleaned inside out. For the first time in my life I am a free man – free of sin, free of the filth that has been inside me for years. The truth has made me free, the truth being our Lord Jesus Christ.

That is a remarkable testimony from a man who wrote from prison. But it highlights the experience every Christian has, of discovering in Christ the power for change. As we grow older we almost despair of change in ourselves. We

99

domesticate our vices: we explain them away to ourselves and to others. We do not expect to see their power snapped. But that is what Jesus Christ can do. 'If the Son makes you free, you will be free indeed', he promised (John 8:36). I think of a proud, arrogant man, now notable for his humility and gentleness since he became a follower of Jesus. I think of a shy, indecisive person who has become calm and resolute. The most obvious changes are seen in fornicators who become chaste, addicts of drink or drugs who are set free, bitter people who become filled with love.

The ability to endure suffering is an area where, for most of us, our self-control is weakest. But here again Christ holds the key. Richard Wurmbrand is a notable example. This Rumanian pastor was for fourteen years imprisoned by the communists for his preaching, and for much of the time he was held below ground in solitary confinement. 'I have seen Christians in communist prisons with fifty pounds of chains on their feet, tortured with red-hot pokers, in whose throats spoonfuls of salt have been forced, being kept afterwards without water, starving, whipped, suffering from cold, and praying with fervour for the communists. It is humanly inexplicable! It is the love of Christ which was shed into our hearts.' Wurmbrand himself had four of his vertebrae smashed, and suffered eighteen holes cut or burnt into his body. Yet he tells us, 'Alone in my cell, cold, hungry and in rags, I danced for joy every night.' He asked another prisoner, whom he had previously led to Christ and was now in prison, whose family was near starvation. 'Have you any resentment against me that I brought you to Christ and because of this your family is in such misery?' The man replied, 'I have no words to express my thankfulness that you have brought me to the wonderful Saviour. I would never have it another way.' Let those who do not need such moral power steer clear of Jesus Christ. I know I could not do without him.

Guilt

Guilt is the last area I propose to mention where Jesus Christ makes the most radical of all differences. Guilt is universal. It is the skeleton in every cupboard, and if you tell me you have no awareness of guilt I shall take leave to doubt your word: the alternative would be to regard you as sub-human. For every human being has a conscience, and for every human being it is an accusing conscience. The theologian Emil Brunner once wrote:

> The bad conscience is like a dog which is shut up in the cellar on account of its tiresome habit of barking, but is continually on the watch to break into the house which is barred against him, and is able to do so the moment the master's vigilance is relaxed. The bad conscience is always there: it is chronic.

Yes, it is there, and it is chronic. Our conscience is not a perfect replica of the voice of God: it gets distorted, like everything else in a fallen world, and we sometimes feel guilty about trivial things whilst neglecting major failures. But it is an uncomfortable reminder to us all that we are responsible beings and that we fail to live up to our responsibilities. We have failed, and do fail daily. We desperately need to have those guilty stains removed. And there is one place, and one only, in the whole world where that is possible.

No other faith offers us any hope in this area. We are either told that we must work our passage to heaven by the good deeds which will (we hope) counterbalance our evil ones; or we are told our failures do not matter (though we know quite well that they do). Or perhaps we are told that evil and its consequent suffering for ourselves and others is unreal (when we know quite well it is nothing of the sort). There is nobody who looks into the depths of the evil in man's heart and says 'I will deal with that' except Jesus Christ. It cost him dear. For he could not simply wave it away. He, and he alone, took personal responsibility on the cross of Calvary for the sins of the whole world. They crushed the life out of him. He cried, in the anguish of a condemned soul, 'My God, why have you forsaken me?' As Peter perceived, 'He bore our sins in his own body on the tree . . .

He once suffered for sins, the just for the unjust, to bring us to God' (1 Peter 2:24; 3:18).

Can we deserve it? Never! That is why Christians are so full of praise and worship to their Saviour. Was it fair? Yes and no. No, in the sense that whenever I receive a gift I could never deserve it. It is not fairness but free, generous love which I experience. But yes, it is fair because Jesus Christ was both God and man. As man he took responsibility for all the sins of all the sinners who had ever lived, were living then, or ever would live. As God, his infinite sacrifice, once for all, more than atoned for all the finite men and women who would come with gratitude to avail themselves of it. And is it relevant? Ask a drowning man if the lifebelt thrown to him is relevant. Ask a bankrupt if the cancellation of all his debts is relevant. 'There is therefore now no condemnation for those who are in Christ Jesus' (Romans 8:1). Does Christianity make any difference? *It makes all the difference!* And nowhere more than in this matter of guilt. Because Christ bore my sins I need not carry the guilt of them on my soul one moment longer. At the deepest level I am accepted by the one who gave me life, the one who gave his life for me.

> Ransomed, healed, restored, forgiven,
> Who like thee His praise should sing?
> Alleluia! Alleluia!
> Praise the everlasting King.

So sang the old hymn-writer. Every Christian can say 'Amen'.

13
Is Christianity dull?

'Christianity? No thanks. Too dull for me.' That is a common objection, and one with which I have a lot of sympathy. For, undeniably, a great deal that passes for Christianity is dull. It seems to be a matter of Sunday best and hymn-singing, of clergy and solemnity, of do's and don'ts — especially don'ts. No wonder a lot of young people are unimpressed.

A group of us from our church were dancing down by the river the other day when the Oxford races were on; we were using short dramatic sketches. We were telling people about the Jesus who came to make life full, not dull. I was talking to one young man who worked in a car factory, and was out with his friends and their cans of beer in the afternoon's sun to have a good time. It amazed him to find a bunch of happy, outward-going Christians enjoying and commending Jesus in the open air at the carnival-like function. That didn't fit in with his image at all. He had attended one church for a while as a lad. 'But I left. It was so dull.'

His only other brush with the church had been when, complete with two children, he had asked to be married. One vicar would not do it. The other would. He thought it rather odd.

There are many like that young man. The church look. dull, restrictive and divided. Alas, it often seems that way, and we who are Christians have a lot to answer for. Very often people are interested and challenged by Jesus, but they are so unimpressed by the church that they keep a safe distance.

The trouble is that in the West the church has got heavily institutionalized and middle-aged. It has become fat and effete. Sheer length of time has something to do with it: a movement can easily lose steam after nineteen hundred years in a country, as Christianity has been in Britain. The establishment has something to do with it: there was a single church in Britain long before there was a single realm; hence the links between church and state. These may be appreciated on state occasions such as the coronation, but they make the church part of the establishment, and to many the establishment is dull by definition.

But if you went to Nigeria or Singapore, to the south of the Sudan or the hills of India, nobody would imagine that Christianity is dull. No state church. No dark suits and pipe organs! The church is very much alive. Often, as in Chile, it is the one adventurous body left in a society that is far from free. Often, as in Russia, it embodies the most courageous and free spirits in the whole of the nation. Often, as in Bolivia, it is the heir to the radical reform for which Ché Guevara lived and died. There is nothing dull about it. So let us make no mistake: dullness is no necessary part of Christianity. The charge would amaze most people, Christian or non-Christian, in the third world. It would amaze many people in Europe and North America too, who have found in Jesus Christ a fullness of life they had never dreamed of before meeting him. It would certainly have amazed the world into which Christianity burst in the thirties of the first century. They had lots of words for Christianity. But they did not call it dull!

There is nothing dull about Jesus

He is the most attractive person the world has ever seen. More books have been written about him, more music composed in his honour, more art directed towards him than any other person in history. Two thousand years after his death he is not merely remembered as the leader of mankind's progress; he is worshipped by hundreds of millions of people all over the world. No minute in the day goes by without men, women and children of all nations singing his praises and

104

expressing their allegiance to him.

In an age when people regarded possessions as the mark of God's blessing, he was penniless and did not wish it other-wise. In days when people thought the acquisition of wealth one of the most important things in life, he told them that it was more blessed to give than to get – and acted accordingly. In an age when there was more class consciousness than in India – or Britain, Jesus made a point of being with the out-casts of society just as much as with the top people. You find him among the prostitutes and tax crooks, among the un-touchable lepers and the ignorant masses, just as much as among the Pharisees and Sadducees. He had no time for formalism or hypocrisy, for washing ceremoniously before dinner or wearing special clothes to eat it. He appealed to rich and poor, Jew and Gentile, men and women alike. He proved supremely attractive to all types. In the Gospels we find an aristocrat like the rich young ruler, a top politician like Nicodemus, a prostitute, a tax gatherer, a variety of women, a crowd of tough fishermen, a mystic like John, a bluff man of action like Peter, political irreconcilables like Judas and Matthew, a dying thief, his executioner, all falling under the spell of this remarkable person. Nobody thought him dull. They might think him dangerous, subversive, radi-cal – but nobody thought him dull. He was vibrantly alive. When he said 'I have come that you may have life in all its fullness', those words were remembered. They rang true.

There is nothing dull about his teaching

No boring do's and don'ts. No long sermons with 'My text is taken from the seventeenth verse of the eighteenth chapter . . .', but memorable, powerful stuff delivered for the most part in the open air. See that man sowing his field over there? Well, listen . . . And there follows the parable of the sower. See those characters fishing out there? The kingdom of heaven is like a great net . . . Do you doubt that God cares about you? See that man selling sparrows in the market, two a penny or five for twopence? Well, your heavenly Father cares about the odd sparrow thrown in for good measure.

You can be sure he cares about you. You are worth many sparrows.

They had never heard anything like it. People did not preach in the open air, but in synagogues. And the learned rabbis kept quoting all the authorities to back up their statements. He said simply, 'Amen (truly) I say to you.' His words had the ring of truth about them.

But they were not comfortable, let alone dull. He told them bad news. He told them that they could never get God in their pocket. That their circumcision, their church-going, their law-keeping could never make them right with God, because he is absolutely holy and perfect, and cannot bear to have evil in his presence. Kind and generous though he was, Jesus nevertheless unveiled, as nobody had done so devastatingly before him, the wickedness of the human heart. 'From within, out of the heart of man, come evil thoughts, fornication, theft, murder, adultery, coveting, wickedness, deceit, licentiousness, envy, slander, pride, foolishness. All these evil things come [not from circumstances over which we have no control, but] from within, and they defile a man' (Mark 7:21ff.).

This recognition of the fundamental twist in human nature (so vociferously and so fatuously denied in progressive modern circles) comes out quite casually in phrases such as, 'If you then, who are evil, know how to give good gifts to your children' (Matthew 7:11). It emerges in stories such as the son who deliberately went on the run from his father's home with half the family fortune, to waste his life with corrupt companions in a foreign country. It blazes out in his scorching denunciation of people's false motives in fasting, praying or giving to God. It appears, with breath-taking candour, in his condemnation of the lustful look as the source of adultery or the bitter word as the origin of murder.

Yet man is not junk. God has not despaired of us. And it is Jesus who gives us the most amazing insight into not only the holiness but also the heart of God. He is like the father in that story of the runaway boy who scans the horizon daily, waiting for the lad to return, and when he does, lacerated, exhausted and ashamed, there is no word of condemnation;

instead the best robe, the fatted calf, and a party. Yes, a party. Do you have that image of God? He throws parties for his rebel subjects when they come back to him!

There are several such stories in the Gospels. In Luke 14 God is portrayed as the host who holds an enormous party and sends round a message at dinner time to the guests saying, 'Come; for all is now ready.' Amazingly, they all begin to make excuses. Very modern, is it not? Eventually the party is furnished with the most unlikely set of guests: not the original folk, who declined to make use of their invitation, but the hungry, the street people, the unemployed. And Matthew makes a most important point in a similar story which he records. Nobody gets through the door into that banqueting-hall until he has exchanged his clothes (be they never so grand or never so tatty) for a wedding garment, provided for him by the host. Nobody need be ashamed now; nobody could afford to boast. All are decked out in a wedding garment they did nothing to deserve. All are accepted at precisely the same level. One man, however, managed to push in wearing his own clothes. And Jesus says that when the king came in to see the guests he noticed this man; the fellow stood out like a sore thumb. And he had him removed from the party. Why? Because he thought his own clothes were good enough. They may be for an ordinary party. But not for God's banquet. Nobody is going to get into heaven flaunting his own goodness. The very idea is revolting. The kingdom of heaven does not consist of self-made men and women but of people who have accepted the fact that, though guilty, they are freely accepted and generously clothed by the king.

Pretty revolutionary stuff, yes? Scarcely dull?

There is nothing dull about his claims

Jesus is often patronized: 'Yes, he's a great moral teacher, but no more.' That position is totally untenable to anyone who takes even a cursory look at the New Testament. It simply won't wash. Jesus made such staggering claims about himself that, if they are untrue, he clearly can't be a good moral teacher, or indeed a good person at all.

1. *He claimed to teach the truth with finality.* 'You have heard that it was said to the men of old, "You shall not kill." But I say to you . . .' 'Heaven and earth will pass away, but my words will not pass away.' 'I have come into the world, to bear witness to the truth. Every one who is of the truth hears my voice.'[1]

2. *He claimed to be able to forgive sins.* 'Jesus said to the paralytic, "My son, your sins are forgiven." Now some of the scribes were sitting there, questioning in their hearts. "Why does this man speak thus? It is blasphemy! Who can forgive sins but God alone?" And Jesus . . . said, ". . . the Son of man has authority on earth to forgive sins."'[2]

3. *He claimed he would judge the world.* 'When the Son of man comes in his glory, and all the angels with him, then he will sit on his glorious throne. Before him will be gathered all the nations, and he will separate them one from another as a shepherd separates the sheep from the goats.' 'On that day many will say to me, "Lord, Lord, did we not prophesy in your name, and cast out demons in your name, and do many mighty works in your name?" And then will I declare to them, "I never knew you; depart from me, you evildoers."' 'The Father judges no one, but has given all judgment to the Son, that all may honour the Son, even as they honour the Father.'[3]

4. *He claimed to be able to satisfy the deepest longings of the human heart.* 'Come to me, all who labour and are heavy laden, and I will give you rest.' 'If any one thirst, let him come to me and drink.' 'I am the bread of life.'[4]

5. *He claimed to be God's Son.* 'All things have been delivered to me by my Father; and no one knows the Son except the Father, and no one knows the Father except the Son and any one to whom the Son chooses to reveal him.' 'No one comes to the Father, but by me.' 'I and the Father are one.' 'The high priest asked him, "Are you the Christ, the

[1] Matthew 5:21ff.; Mark 13:31; John 18:37.
[2] Mark 2:5–10.
[3] Matthew 25:31f.; 7:22f.; John 5:22f.
[4] Matthew 11:28; John 7:37; 6:35.

Son of the Blessed?" And Jesus said, "I am; and you will see the Son of man sitting at the right hand of Power, and coming with the clouds of heaven."'[5]

6. *He claimed the right to receive worship.* Men should 'honour the Son, even as they honour the Father'. When Thomas doubted the reality of Jesus' resurrection, Jesus invited him to touch his wounds and assure himself. He fell at the feet of Jesus saying, 'My Lord and my God!' Jesus did not rebuke him for this supreme act of worship; gently he chides him for not having done it until then. This stands in striking contrast to a couple of occasions in the Acts of the Apostles when simple people offered divine worship to Peter and to Paul. Both repudiated it with horror. 'Why are you doing this?' asked Paul. 'We also are men, of like nature with you, and bring you good news, that you should turn from these vain things to the living God.'[6] Yet Jesus calmly accepted worship as his due.

There is nothing dull about such a person. He forces us into a place where we must decide. He is utterly unlike any other religious teacher. Nobody else ever made claims remotely comparable to these. What are we to make of them?

The really foolish thing that people say about him is that 'I'm ready to accept him as a great moral teacher, but I don't accept his claim to be God.' A man who is merely a man and said the sort of things Jesus said would not be a great moral teacher. He would either be a lunatic – on a level with a man who says he is a poached egg – or else he would be the devil of hell. You must make your choice. Either this man was and is the Son of God: or else a madman, or something worse. (C. S. Lewis.)

There is nothing dull about his achievement

The achievement of Jesus is measureless. Let me isolate merely three elements in it.

[5] Matthew 11:27, John 14:6; 10:30; Mark 14:61f.
[6] John 5:23; 20:26ff.; Acts 10:25f.; 14:15.

First, the new standing it makes possible. Jesus once told a remarkable little story. It concerned a Pharisee, a most punc-
tilious man of religion. He went into the temple to pray. And
he told God all the good things he had done. There was also
present the classic bad guy of the day, a publican. He simply
cried out in profound humility and repentance, 'God, be
merciful to me, bad man that I am.' And Jesus said that bad
man went home 'justified', acquitted, right with God (Luke
18:9–14). How come? How is it possible for the moral ruler
of the universe to be merciful to one who had so flouted his
laws? Because of what Jesus was about to achieve on the
cross. There he took full responsibility for the manifold guilt
of that publican, and of everyone else. It was the most amazing rescue in all history. Jesus repeatedly said he had come to
give his life as a ransom for many (*e.g.* Mark 10:45). He did
just that. Our lives were forfeit; for sin cuts us off from enjoying the life of God. But Christ offered his life up in place of
our forfeit lives. He paid our bills to the last cent, and he
gasped out that achievement with almost his last breath,
'*Tetelestai*, it is finished, it is paid' (John 19:30).

No wonder Paul got so excited about that word 'justified'.
He saw that this acquittal which God confers on those who
trust him, this acquittal which had been purchased at such a
cost on Calvary, has always been the way by which God can
welcome sinful men back into his company. That is how
Abraham was accepted, and David and Moses. They trusted
in the God who acquits the ungodly. And although they did
not know about Calvary, God did. He knew that he would
find a way to achieve that infinitely costly ransom. So it is not
a question of the goodies and the baddies and a vast mob in
between; it never has been. It is a question of whether or not
we have accepted God's verdict of 'guilty' on ourselves, and
have allowed ourselves to be touched by those outstretched
arms of Jesus crucified, which whisper to us 'justified'.
'Therefore, since we are justified by faith, we have peace
with God through our Lord Jesus Christ' (Romans 5:1).

Second, the new power it makes available. Jesus Christ did not
stay in that tomb. He rose from the dead. And the implications of that are enormous. It means he is indeed the Son of

110

God, as he claimed during his earthly life. It means he has opened the door to eternal life for all who love him. It means that evil does not have the last word in God's world. It means above all that the very power which raised Christ from the dead is available to us, if we get in touch with him. Paul prays that his friends at Ephesus will have their eyes opened to 'the immeasurable greatness of his power in us who believe, according to the working of his great might which he accomplished in Christ when he raised him from the dead' (Ephesians 1:19f.). That resurrection power of Christ is let loose in the lives of Christians. Jesus brings it with him into their lives, once he is welcomed in. No wonder then that moral revolution often follows conversion. It always should. When it does not, this is because we refuse to accept his mighty power; we prefer to stay as we are. And the Lord is grieved, because he wants the best for us. But he will not force us, for love does not force. Instead, he gently calls us (or maybe strongly challenges us) to allow his resurrection power to change us. The resurrection of Jesus has opened up an entirely new set of options in our lives.

It is no good giving me a play like Hamlet or King Lear, and telling me to write a play like that. Shakespeare could do it; I can't. And it is no good showing me a life like the the life of Jesus and telling me to live a life like that. Jesus could do it; I can't. But if the genius of Shakespeare could come and live in me, then I could write plays like that. And if the Spirit of Jesus could come and live in me, I could live a life like that. (William Temple.)

The good news is that the Spirit of Jesus *can* come into us, and all the power that raised him from the dead is available to break in us the habits which have chained us for so long.

Third, the community it has launched. Part of the achievement of Jesus is that he has inaugurated the greatest fan club in history. He has founded a community of people of all ages, types and nationalities, who are entrusted with the most exciting adventure imaginable. They are asked to model a new life-style. They are meant to be the outriders of the kingdom of God. They are intended to be Christ's commandos in enemy-occupied territory. They are called to be a society bound together by love in the midst of a world that is falling apart. The church is part of the gospel. The church is part of Christ's achievement. Alas, it is often spineless and worldly, dull and incompetent, selfish and divided. That is when it does not allow the power of the risen Christ to transform its personal and corporate life. That is when it is untrue to the charter of its founder. But mercifully the church, and the individuals in it, do sometimes draw on the resources of their Father, and they do live a different kind of life in the midst of a godless society. When this happens people sit up and take notice. Because it is not dull: it is immensely attractive. 'And when they had prayed, the place in which they were gathered together was shaken; and they were all filled with the Holy Spirit and spoke the word of God with boldness. Now the company of believers were of one heart and soul, and no one said that any of the things which he possessed was his own, but they had everything in common. And with great power the apostles gave their testimony to the resurrection of the Lord Jesus, and great grace was upon them all.' That was Luke's thumb-nail sketch of some of the earliest Christians (Acts 4:31ff.). He makes it plain in the story of Ananias and Sapphira, which follows, that it was not all like that, even in those early days. But what a society, this Society of Jesus! When it lives like its founder, everything is possible. And nothing is dull . . .

There is nothing dull about his challenge

Unlike many teachers, Jesus did not send people away to write essays. He himself never wrote a book. He did not offer them good advice, nor submit his views for their consideration.

He came to them with an intrinsic authority, the authority of dynamic teaching and a perfect life. He practised what he preached. He demonstrated his love for them all the way to the cross, and even there he was pleading for the forgiveness of his torturers. He fully earned the right to speak. And he

112

said, 'Come to me,' 'Follow me,' 'Lay down your life for me.'

Nothing dull about that. Totally adventurous. To commit oneself without reserve to the most perfect, the most exciting person the world has ever seen. Not dull. But very costly. And there's the rub.

I believe we often fight shy of Christianity because we fear it will make us dull. It will do nothing of the kind. It will make us holy, and that is a very different thing, a very attractive thing, but a very costly thing. We draw back, because we are afraid of the cost.

Yes, it is undeniably costly to follow Jesus. He made this abundantly plain on many occasions, but never more so than after he had spoken of God's great supper party, open to all and sundry. God offers his all to us all. But he wants all of us in return. And so Jesus goes on in the second part of that chapter, Luke 14, to outline what it will cost to follow him. He asks us, in effect, five questions.

Are you prepared to put him first? (verse 26). He has to come before parents and lovers and every other commitment. He deserves it. He gave everything for us. He is utterly trustworthy. He does not want to rob us of anything that is good in our lives. But he demands total obedience. He must come first. He must be the *Lord* Jesus Christ. Are you ready for that?

Are you prepared to carry your cross? (verse 27). People talk about their bad liver as their cross! But Jesus meant something very different. The cross was a very public thing, a very grisly and painful thing. Are you willing to go public as his follower? You will be laughed at. You will find it heavy and painful on many an occasion. You will at times find yourself crushed by it. But he carried it for you. He died on it for you. Are you prepared to follow him in sacrifice, yes, and in suffering? Are you prepared to start by telling someone else you are going to follow Jesus? That's the crunch . . . to start with. The cross cuts deeper later on.

Are you prepared to keep going? (verse 28). Don't be like the man who built a 'folly' because he hadn't reckoned up what it would cost to complete the job. It is not a hasty commitment you are being asked for. Jesus wants your lifelong alle-

113

giance. He is not looking for decisions. He wants disciples. Are you ready for that?

Are you prepared for a struggle? (verse 31). Jesus talked of going to war if you follow him. It means declaring war on the greed and lust and selfishness in yourself, for a start, and letting him deal with them. The job will never be finished in this life, but it will be a progressive victory. Then it means being willing to enlist with Christ against the forces of evil in society. It will call for integrity, courage, unpopularity at times. Are you ready for that?

Are you prepared to be in a minority? (verses 31–32). Not very pleasant, is it? But Jesus realistically said you would need to work it out and see if with 10,000 troops you dare confront someone who comes against you with 20,000. It's like that in the Christian life. Always in a minority, because so many others have not seen Christ's light yet, or, having seen it, have not had the courage to come to him.

No, there's nothing dull about Jesus, or his challenge. The question is, have we the courage to put our lives at his disposal, or shall we stay on the run?

DECISION

14
On the run...?

The polls show that more than three-quarters of the people of Great Britain claim to believe in a personal God. In the U.S.A. it is far more. But how many of them do anything about him? In a crisis, maybe, or when a close relative appears to be dying. The odd wedding in church. Christmas and Easter in the congregation, perhaps. But there it ends — unless we persist in the habit, learnt from mother, of saying the same few prayers before we go to bed.

There is in fact a widespread retreat from religion in Western Europe at the present time, though Christianity is burgeoning in America and Africa, the Far East and many Communist lands. What accounts for this retreat? Undoubtedly the church is partly responsible. It has often been defensive, inward-looking, lacking in social concern and devoid of clear and relevant preaching to ordinary people about the great issues of life and death. The church has gone a long way towards making Christianity incredible.

But when this has been said, and it must be said with deep humility by any thoughtful Christian, the current drift away from Christianity is culpable. Lots of folk who are willing to dismiss religion with a wave of the hand are themselves unwilling to face up to the evidence for Jesus and the challenge of his person. If Christianity is wrong about God and man, our origin and destiny, the value of persons and the secret of living together in community, then get up and say so. But say it after you have examined the evidence. That seems perfectly obvious, and yet that is precisely what many are appar-

115

ently too afraid or too lazy to do. On matters of such importance they are content to be guided by scraps of information
gleaned long ago in the Sunday School, by the latest newspaper attack on the faith, or by the voice and visiting habits
of the local clergy.

Modern apathy about Christianity is often sheer escapism.
People are afraid of what facing up to the challenge of Jesus
might mean. Have you noticed how people avoid sitting next
to the man in the dog-collar in bus or train? How some of
the most militant atheists in the university simply dare not
go along to a Christian meeting? How many a working man
is literally terrified of being seen entering a church?

Behind all these attitudes lies fear. Fear of having to be
reminded of the God we would much rather forget. Fear
of having our lives scrutinized and spring-cleaned by God. Fear
of what others might say if we came out on the side of Jesus
Christ. So it is much easier, much more comfortable, to run
away.

Blind alleys

There are many forms of escapism. It does not always spring
from a conscious attempt to run away from God. Often it is the
mess the world is in, or the mess our lives are in, which puts us
on the run.

Sex is probably the commonest way of getting away from
it all. You have only to glance at television, or read the walls
of in the New York subway where advertisement
after advertisement shouts at you, 'Sex satisfies. Sex is the
way to fulfilment.' Quite apart from the old favourites like
pre-marital sex and adultery, there has been a considerable
diversification in recent years. Male and female homosexuality
has become the rage. Sex is presented to us as a therapy, a sport,
a gourmet diet. Pornography in films and erotic magazines has
spread enormously. Sex shops spring up in even small towns.
Films almost require an X certificate to get an audience. Virgins
are a dying breed. The great myth has triumphed: turn to sex
and all will be well.

But of course we know that all is not well. Unhappiness in

116

the home seems to be on the increase rather than the reverse. Wives unaccountably do not seem to like it when their husbands sleep around. AIDS has risen sharply, and abortions are a roaring trade. We talk primly about the foetus not being a person before the 26th week, or whatever our preference is. But what we mean is, 'Leave me alone to have sex as and when I will. If we make a mistake, too bad. We can get an abortion.' How is this attitude of violence to the defenceless affecting our national and personal character? What is lack of restraint doing to us? How about the families that are sickened by extra-marital relations and broken through divorce? What happens to the children? The answer is simple. They are robbed of the love of one or both parents. They feel betrayed. Many of them contribute to one of the fastest-growing industries in the west — the teenage crime wave in the under-16s.

Drugs remain high on the list of escape routes for those on the run. I include the hard stuff, the heroin and cocaine, but they are rather less popular these days, for they are recognized widely for the killers they are. But the tranquillizers which are ceaselessly dispensed by the family doctor, the pep pills, the anti-depressants, the smoking habit and above all the rapidly increasing consumption of alcohol, the most dangerous (and socially acceptable) drug of them all — all of these things are profoundly disturbing. They show the pressures of modern life. They show how desperate people are to alleviate those pressures, even if the escape route imposes its own bondage — or perhaps death.

Eastern religions are very much in vogue. The sixties was the age of the radical protest. The hippie counter-culture failed, and many of the radicals of those days have switched to the inner revolution of drugs and mysticism which has been such a characteristic of the seventies. Both drugs and Eastern mysticism despair of the external world: man is a machine, God is dead, values are man-made. Instead, both seek meaning within. But you cannot rest there. You cannot find meaning in the sphere of the non-rational. The journey within is pure escapism, and it will not satisfy.

Transcendental meditation has a great following. What welcome relief from the pressures of modern society! This too comes from the East. It is basically Hindu in its inspiration and in the deities to which the teachers give allegiance in their initiation. And that has its dangers. Moreover such meditation stands in striking contrast to Christian mysticism which draws people into a deep relationship with the personal, loving God, and then sends them back into the world to love others with his love. There is nothing selfish about it. By contrast, TM is essentially self-related. A correspondence to a national newspaper put this point very forcibly:

> No wonder that those who meditate feel peaceful, simple and calm. Disregard the world about you and you have nothing to worry about. It is this self-abstraction which is the product of meditation that has landed India in its present state of semi-starvation. Five thousand years of meditation have never ploughed a field or built a house.

All too often the meditator is on the run.

There are plenty of other escape routes. *Television* is a prime one. Come back home, sit down, switch off from the world and on to the box for a few hours, and then go to bed. Good for escaping bad for personal relationships.

Violence is a fashionable escape route for some to whom the grim realities of life spell utter poverty, racial discrimination, or unemployment. It is often action without manifesto, a desperate attempt to draw attention to oneself. In the end, it is self-destructive.

Conformism is another cop-out. We just do what everyone else does and feel that in such company we must be all right. Church-going may even fall into the same category. Ask some people why they do it and they will tell you, "It makes me feel good.' It is the religious person's rabbit-hole into which he bolts each week.

Two of the most popular escape routes are apathy and the rat-race. *Apathy* is the most common attitude among young

118

rat-race. *Apathy* is the most common attitude among young people in the West today, and it stands in striking contrast to the enthusiasm and determination to get on which marks young people in the third world. Where in Britain or U.S.A. would they camp outside a school in the hope of getting a place if someone fell out? The 'why bother?' syndrome has become the English disease. And it is very malignant. A nation is in a poor way when it has ceased to bother. An individual is in a serious state when he looks at the greatest offer and the greatest person in the world and shrugs his shoulders with an implied 'So what?'. I find it very hard to admire such an attitude. It lacks integrity: the apathetic man does not want to look at evidence which might challenge him to act. He'd rather stay with his head in the sand. It is cowardly: to sit on the fence over the really significant issues shows you are on the run from truth. And it is ungrateful: if Jesus Christ really did come to this world and live and die and rise again for the likes of us, then apathy is inexcusable. 'Couldn't care less' is a particularly disreputable escape route from the challenges of life at the end of the 20th century.

The rat-race can often be an escape route too. Get out of school into a well-paid job. Get more money each year, and better prospects. Get a husband or wife, a car and a house. Get a family, a better house and a second car. Get promotion. Get ulcers. Get a good pension. And then fill your life up with as much as you can before you die. Whatever you do, don't allow yourself to wonder what life is all about. It might be too depressing a question. I heard a celebrated broadcaster express this attitude with great candour. 'I erect a wall of busyness around me. I remember Jonathan Miller once saying he did not like not being busy in case nasty thoughts of death and the eternal verities started to creep up on him. I'm rather the same.'

A great many people, especially men, make work their bolt-hole, though when you set it down in cold print it looks a peculiarly foolish brand of escapism. Yet those who adopt this irresponsible attitude are often the ones who maintain, over their gin and tonic with a colleague, that it is the Christians who are on the run!

Stop!

Whichever of these blind alleys we choose, Jesus Christ stands there, barring the way, with his arms outstretched. He calls on us to stop running away, and to start running with him. We shall not, in any case, succeed in getting away from that man with his cross. One day we shall meet him face to face. We shall be assessed by the ideal man, the supreme lover, from whom we have been running away all our lives. What convincing excuses shall we have to offer for our evasions? 'I didn't believe you existed'? What culpable neglect of the evidence! 'There were too many hypocrites in church'? Why, then, did you not take pains to ally yourself with the one who is truth? 'There was too much suffering in the world'? I know, he will reply: I bore it. 'I was afraid'? Ah, but you should have come to me. Perfect love casts out fear. You remained chained to fear because you rejected my love. Or shall we simply have to admit, 'I did not bother'? How threadbare that will look to the Son of God who loved you and gave himself for you.

Our excuses will all wither away before the love, the truth, the self-sacrifice of Jesus. There will come a final day of reckoning, and our relationship with him will prove decisive. It will be crystal clear then what answer we have returned to Pilate's crucial question, 'What shall I do with Jesus?' For, as the Good Book reminds us, 'it is appointed for men to die once, and after that comes judgment' (Hebrews 9:27).

15
... Or in the race?

The metaphor of the race is one the New Testament writers were quite fond of, and none more so than Saul of Tarsus. He knew all about being on the run. He was running away from his conscience which had been convicted by the life and death of Stephen. After all, he had been an accomplice at his murder. So to still his conscience he ran hard and fast in the opposite direction, and started persecuting the Christians. A lot of people react like that, once they realize Jesus is the truth but are not prepared to give in to him.

So Paul continued on the run for a while. And then Jesus caught up with him. The Christ he dared not face but could not escape confronted him on the road near Damascus. Saul stopped running. He fell to the ground. He realized what a fool he had been. He recognized, perhaps for the first time in his life, that Jesus was not a heretic dead and gone, but a Saviour alive and well. He realized with deep shame that he had been persecuting not merely the Christians but Jesus as well. He then and there surrendered to him. For Saul, that was the beginning of a new life. 'If any one is in Christ, he is a new creature,' he wrote later on; 'the old has passed away, behold, the new has come' (2 Corinthians 5:17).

It may be that you, like Saul, have been on the run. Like him you are ready for a change. You too would like to join the Christian race. What would it mean?

You must begin

Nobody just drifts into a race. You have to enrol. You have to come under starter's orders. You have to abide completely by what he directs. He positions you. He fires the pistol to start you off. Hebrews 12:2 sees Jesus as the Starter. You cannot enter the Christian race without coming under his orders. What are they?

Jesus' first word to us is '*Repent*'. It comes many times in the New Testament. It does not mean weeping crocodile tears for our sins: it does mean turning away from them. I used to imagine that I had to clean my life up before I could expose it to Jesus' gaze. No, repentance is just opening up the house, so to speak, and inviting him to clear out the rubbish. Of course, the supreme thing to repent of is the way we have treated God: we have left him out of account and turned our back on his call. Repentance is therefore sometimes called 'repentance towards God' in the Bible. It means a change of attitude. Instead of leaving him out we start including him in.

Jesus' second word to us is '*Believe*'. That, too, can easily be misunderstood. It involves not merely the assent of our minds but the trust of our hearts. It is not intellectual suicide: it is the thoughtful commitment of our whole selves to Jesus who has shown his reliability right up to death – and beyond. Nor does it mean that we are expected to swallow at one gulp everything in the Bible or in various Christian formulations throughout the centuries. 'Believe in me,' he says, or, 'Believe in the good news.' He *is* the good news! The good news that God cares for us so much that he has come to find us; that he has not allowed our failures to alienate him, but has himself dealt with them once and for all on the cross; and that he is alive again, willing and able to share our lives if we will let him. That is what we are asked to do: commit ourselves in total trust to such a Lord.

Jesus' third word to us is '*Come*'. 'Come to me, all who are heavy laden,' he says, 'and I will give you rest' (Matthew 11:28). On another occasion he laments, 'You refuse to come to me that you may have life' (John 5:40). To come is a very basic idea. We all know what it means to come home, to come to a loved one, to come to a meal. Well, Jesus is our home from whom we have long strayed. He is our lover who agonizes for our return. He is the sustenance of our souls and he longs to feed us. Come, he says, *you* come! Well, why not? Coming is very simple, but it can have enormous consequences. He said 'Come' to Simon Peter, and it changed his whole life. 'Come after me and I will make you a fisher of men.' It happened. The same sort of change could happen to you . . . *if you will come.*

Why not lay the book down now, wherever you are, and come back to the Lord? Say to him in your own words that you are sorry to have kept out of his way for so long, sorry you have been on the run. Tell him how grateful you are that he died on the cross for you, that he rose again from the tomb, and is alive and able to help. Tell him that you are willing for him to make changes in your life, and you realize that it is going to be costly. If you like, why not use the words of the old hymn-writer?

> Just as I am, without one plea
> But that thy blood was shed for me,
> And that thou bidd'st me come to thee,
>   O Lamb of God, I come.

> Just as I am – thy love unknown
> Has broken every barrier down –
> Now to be thine, yea, thine alone,
>   O Lamb of God, I come.

And Jesus says, 'Him who comes to me I will not cast out' (John 6:37). That 'will not' is a double negative in the Greek. It is very strong. It means 'I will never, no never, cast out'. If you have genuinely come to him, as best as you know how, then he *has* accepted you. You see, he has promised to do so, and he cannot break his word. Therein lies your security.

Jesus' fourth word to us is '*Follow*'. Our decision may well be crystallized in a moment. But following takes a lifetime. We are now launched on the long path of discipleship. And a disciple means a learner. There is a great deal to learn.

You must train

You never get anywhere in a race unless you train. It is just not possible. The same is true in the Christian life. Without training we get puffed and give up in next to no time. 'Every athlete is disciplined in all things,' says the apostle Paul. 'I pommel my body and subdue it' (1 Corinthians 9:25–27). He was writing to the Corinthians, where the famous Isthmian Games were held. They understood the imagery well. But what, in practical terms, does this training mean?

Well, think of any athlete. How does he train? He does without things which are injurious to him, such as alcohol, cigarettes and late nights, and he builds up muscle. The Christian needs discipline too.

There are certain things which are injurious to us. They differ with different people. Certain relationships, certain places, certain habits which are no good for us. And Jesus says to us, like a good coach, 'Cut those out. Get fit.' But unlike any human coach, he actually enables us to remove them from our lives. He offers us not merely the diagnosis of what is injurious to us, but the power to deal with it. So get into the habit from the start of your discipleship of offering your day to the Lord when you get up in the morning. Ask him to show you any problem areas, and to enable you to look to him for help when the need arises. Get into the habit of saying under your breath to him, 'Lord, give me the power to overcome that one'; and you will find he will. It is exhilarating to find a power not your own working away inside you, dealing with those weaknesses and excesses which render you unfit for the race.

But training is not merely a case of saying No. The athlete needs to build up his body. So it is in the Christian race. There are three ways in particular whereby we can be built up and nourished.

One is the Holy Communion, the meal Jesus left us so that we could not merely remember his death for us, but feed on him, draw on his resources in our hearts as we trust him. You may or may not be baptized and in membership of any church. If you are not, it is something to sort out. And then you will be welcomed to the family meal of the Christians, the Holy Communion. It is one of the great ways to grow.

Another is the Bible. 'Desire the pure spiritual milk, that by it you may grow up to salvation; for you have tasted the kindness of the Lord,' said Peter (1 Peter 2:2–3). And the Bible gives us that spiritual milk . . . and, for that matter, the strong meat, once we have grown our teeth. If you take any subject seriously you want to read about it. If you take any friendship seriously you want to read what that person writes to you. For both these reasons you need to read the Bible. It will shed light on your path as a Christian. It will deepen your friendship with your Lord.

So get hold of some system to help you; there are several good ones. *Food for Life*, *Search the Scriptures*, the *Scripture Union Notes*, or *Every Day with Jesus* all have their enthusiastic adherents. It might be wise to find a Christian friend and ask his advice on how to go about it.

A third way to grow is prayer. The coach and the athlete are in constant communication. That is what our relationship with Jesus is meant to be like. Not that we can be praying *all* the time. But we can pray at *any* time. That is the point. Be ready to turn to him at any moment in the day with a 'thank you', a 'sorry' or a 'please'. But here again prayer is something we all need to grow into. We never get to the bottom of it, for, after all, it is a relationship with a living person, who is inexhaustible.

You must run the race

'Therefore, since we are surrounded by so great a cloud of witnesses, let us also lay aside every weight, and sin which clings so closely, and let us run with perseverance the race that is set before us, looking to Jesus, the starter and finisher of our faith, who for the joy that was set before him endured the cross, despising the shame, and is seated at the right hand of God.' So wrote the author of the letter to the Hebrews (12:1–2). What a marvellous image! There is the stadium, with the stands full of past competitors, urging on the athletes. Off come the sweaters and track suits, and each one is stripped down to singlet and shorts. They are under starter's orders. Then they are off.

There are a lot of them in the race. It is not a solitary affair, as much of the training perforce must be. Christians need each other. We are not meant to operate on our own in the Christian life.

It is a very public race. You can't go in for something like this and hope to remain unnoticed. So it is with the Christian. You have to be willing to be seen to be in the race and not mind a few laughs or groans.

It is a long-distance race. It lasts a whole lifetime. So take this into account, and plan accordingly. Make sure you pace yourself carefully. Make sure your life-partner is in it too, or you will be slowed down to a crawl.

It is no good looking backwards over your shoulder in the race. You need to keep looking ahead to Jesus. He started you off in this race. He is going to be there at the final tape. He is running it along with you, to encourage you. Look to him when it is uphill and you have got a stitch. Keep your eyes steadily on him and do what he tells you. You will run well.

And remember, you must be determined to finish the race. Hundred-yard sprinters are no use in this marathon. Paul was utterly determined to be there at the finish. 'So run that you may obtain the prize,' he told his friends at Corinth: 'I do not run aimlessly' (1 Corinthians 9:24, 26). And on an occasion towards the end of his life he could look ahead to times of opposition and pain that he knew he would have to go through and say, 'None of these things move me. I do not account my life of any value nor as precious to myself, if only I may finish my course and the ministry which I received from the Lord Jesus, to testify to the gospel of the grace of God' (Acts 20:24). Well, his wish was granted. He ran faith-fully to the end, and for him that meant the executioner's sword on the Appian Way at Rome. Just before that happened a short letter was smuggled out of prison to his lieutenant and son in the faith, Timothy. In it he was able to say, 'I have fought the good fight, *I have finished the race*, I have kept the faith. Henceforward there is laid up for me the crown of righteousness [the victor's wreath], which the Lord, the righteous judge, will award to me on that Day, and not only to me but also to all who love his appearing' (2 Timothy 4:7–8).

What a magnificent prospect for runners who finish the race!

Other Books of Interest

Knowing the Truth of God's Love
Peter Kreeft

God's love is the subject of Peter Kreeft's imaginative and thoughtful new book. With unusual clarity, he points out that the man or woman who begins to glimpse the God who is Redeemer, Creator, and Lover of our souls, will never be the same. He describes Scripture as a love story and then tells why divine love is the answer to our deepest problems. *$8.95*

Knowing the Truth about Heaven and Hell
Harry Blamires

Harry Blamires believes that many people are in danger of forgetting the truth about heaven and hell, to their peril. He points out that our choices have an immense impact upon our eternal well-being—unending happiness with God or the unimaginable sorrow of eternal anguish. *Knowing the Truth about Heaven and Hell* brings you into touch with ultimate realities. It challenges, inspires, and leads us to a deeper understanding of the Father's desire to unite all men and women to himself forever. The invitation is clear. The choice is ours. *$8.95*

Knowing the Truth about the Resurrection
William L. Craig

Did Jesus rise from the dead? Is there proof for the resurrection? Are the accounts in the Gospels of Jesus' burial, the empty tomb, and his resurrection appearances reliable?

William L. Craig candidly addresses these provocative questions and many more. Laying out the arguments, both pro and con, he presents a compelling case for the resurrection as an event of earth-shattering significance for the human race. *$8.95*